THIS BOOK BELONGS TO:

Verses marked NLT are taken from the Holy Bible, New Living Translation, copyright © 1996, 2004, 2007, 2015 by Tynsdale House Foundation. Used by permission of Tyndale House Publishers, Inc., Carol Stream, Illinois 60188. All rights reserved..

Cover by Shelly-Deane Neil

Interior Design by Shelly-Deane Neil

Edited by Christanya Julien

Chosen: I CHOOSE US

Copyright © 2021 by Shelly-Deane Neil (text)

ISBN 978-0-578-88136-2 (hardcover)

All rights reserved. No part of this publication may be reproduced, stored in a retrieval system or transmitted in any form or by any means - electronic ,mechanical, photocopy, recording or any other without the prior written permission of the author.

Printed in China

Chosen: I Choose Us

Shelly-Deane Neil ♥

Contents:

Introduction	1
Chosen: I Choose Us	2
Let Go and Let God	6
Yielding to God	10
New Life	14
Reset	18
Clean Heart	22
Submitting to God	26
Focus on God	30
Time	34
Walking in Faith	38
Living in the Spirit	42
Grace to Embrace	46
Courage	50
Love	54
Forgiveness	58
Discipline	62
Trust	66
Confidence	70

Contents:

Praise Be	……… 74
Calling	……… 78
Higher Purpose	……… 82
Be Still	……… 86
Guidance	……… 90
Protection	……… 94
Blessings	……… 98
Power	……… 102
Obedience	……… 106
Boldness	……… 110
Faith	……… 114
Fruitfulness	……… 118
Reassurance	……… 122
Peace	……… 126
His Presence	……… 130
Good Shepherd	……… 134
Everlasting Joy	……… 138
Claiming God's Promises	……… 142
Worship	……… 146
Believe	……… 150
Child of God	……… 154
Glory to God	……… 158

Declarations:

Child of God	 164
Love	 166
Faith	 168
Peace	 170
Fruit of the Spirit	 172
Guidance	 174
Wisdom	 176
Light	 178
Favor	 180
Victory/Strength	 182
Note Pages	 184
Acknowledegements	 189

How we got here:

Chosen is a beautifully designed prayer book that includes Scripture corresponding to each prayer, guided reflections and a few declarations to speak the word of God over your life.

My prayers are written from the very core of my heart as I am a new born believer who knows the struggle between letting go of your old life and walking into the new life God has planned for you and all in-betweens. This book is intended to inspire people to form and have an intimate relationship with God, to inspire non-believers to draw close to and choose God; and to refresh believers, strengthen their faith and help them to walk in their divine purpose. It covers topics from Letting Go to Submitting unto God to Claiming His promises.

I believe this gift was given to me after my very first three days of fasting. I experienced the presence of God through the Holy Spirit like never before. His peace and love covered me like the warmest, fluffiest most comfortable blanket. My life has completely changed since, and well, there will be no turning back. He chose me and on that very day I made the biggest decision of my life to completely choose Him too.

I knew this meant letting go of my old ways of life, my old ways of thinking and speaking and, not to mention, my old ways of doing. To do this, I needed to know the new way. I needed to know that giving up something meant receiving something better. How better to learn these things than reading the word of God? But, easier said than done right?

I hated reading! - and here I am writing a book. Can you imagine? But through God's grace, I started not only reading the bible but also enjoying it too! I read five chapters a day, choosing Scriptures that stood out to me and writing about what I received from them. I wrote down every Scripture that convicted me, prayed and confessed my wrongs to God and received forgiveness and salvation. Before I knew it, I read all the Books of the New Testament in two months and got started on the Old Testament to get a deeper understanding.

Although my journey is just beginning, I believe God wants to use me to serve others through this book. I wrote it to remind you that you're not alone in this. We all struggle and fall short in one way or another. But through our weaknesses, He is made strong and with Him all things are possible! So what are you waiting for? Buckle up and let's embark on this, at times, overwhelming yet rewarding journey together.

It's worth the read! **STOP**

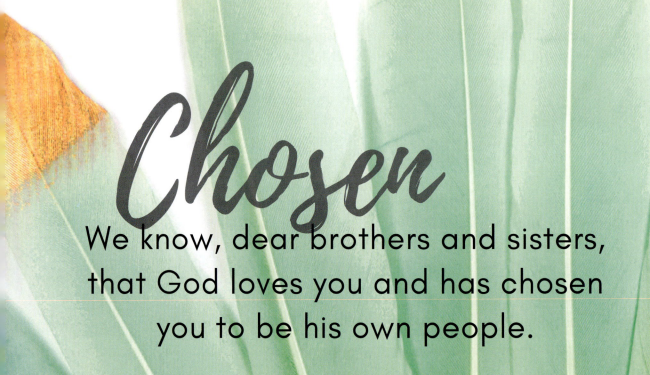

Chosen

We know, dear brothers and sisters, that God loves you and has chosen you to be his own people.

1 THESSALONIANS 1:4 NLT.

CHOSEN: I CHOOSE US

Hello my sweet Jesus, Today I won't pray for anything. I won't ask for anything. Today I just want to praise Your holy name and show my gratitude. Today I only want to thank You! You have blessed me so much that I want to give back to You with my whole heart and all my joy. Thank You for being an awesome God, for knowing all and carrying me through all things. For always speaking and ministering to my heart, knowing exactly what and when I need it. Thank You for Your unconditional and everlasting love. For loving me even when I show that I am far from perfect and undeserving. Thank You for Your Holy Spirit who comforts, intercedes and advocates for me. Thank You for being a God of promises and faithfulness, for believing in me even when I find it impossible to believe in myself. Thank You for Your blessings and breakthroughs, for favoring me and filling me with Your love. Thank You for Your grace that You give so willingly each day. Thank You for being so good to me. Thank You, my God, for Your mercy and compassion that provides promising glints of light in this darkened world. Thank You for Your forgiveness; for allowing Your only Son to bear all my sins on the cross, causing them to depart from me and freeing my heart. Thank You for Your strength and courage to do great things when I am weak and broken. Thank You for being the God of miracles; for never disappointing me but staying true to your word, keeping Your promises and creating ways out of no way. I praise You for being all-powerful, providing supernatural intervention and clearing pathways before me. Thank You that not only are You able, but willing to do exceedingly, abundantly above all I have ever asked, hoped or imagined. Dear God, thank You for giving me a heart to know You and a great desire to see more of You in my life. Thank You for choosing me. I love You, I believe in You and I choose You. I choose us each and every single time. Amen.

Psalm 119:113 nlt.

Give me a helping hand, for I have chosen to follow your commandments.

♥ WHAT AM I GRATEFUL FOR? HAVE I CHOSEN GOD, IF NOT WHAT AM I WAITING FOR?!

Let God

I pray that God, the source of hope, will fill you completely with joy and peace because you trust in him. Then you will overflow with confident hope through the power of the Holy Spirit

Romans 15:13 nlt.

LET GO & LET GOD

"Don't copy the behavior and customs of this world, but let God transform you into a new person by changing the way you think. Then you will learn to know God's will for you, which is good and pleasing and perfect." Romans 12:2

Dear Heavenly and Righteous Father, Today, I pray that You will help me to let go of the things of my past so I can move into a future with You. It can be hard to let go of what seems normal, what I've gotten so accustomed to even if it no longer serves or benefits me. God, help me to release my doubts. Help me to have so much confidence and courage in You that I am willing to let go of all that I have in order to receive all You are giving. Help me to loosen my grip on life, on the things I have no control over, on my expectations and help me to be so trustful in You, to partner with You and not work against You. Shut down everything around me to birth what is within me. Teach me to set my agendas from within and be guided by Your Holy Spirit, fulfilling Your purpose in my life. Set me free from the things I don't need, dear God. As I let go of my past season, teach me the lessons of this season and prepare me for the next. Help me to unlearn the way the world works so I can see how You work. Remove my need to know, dear God, as well as everything in my life that can be shaken. I invite You to come into my life and purge everything that is useless and what is worth keeping, use it for Your glory. Father, I pray that You would let the desires of my heart align with Your will for my life. Help me to let go and let God. In Your holy name I pray, Amen.

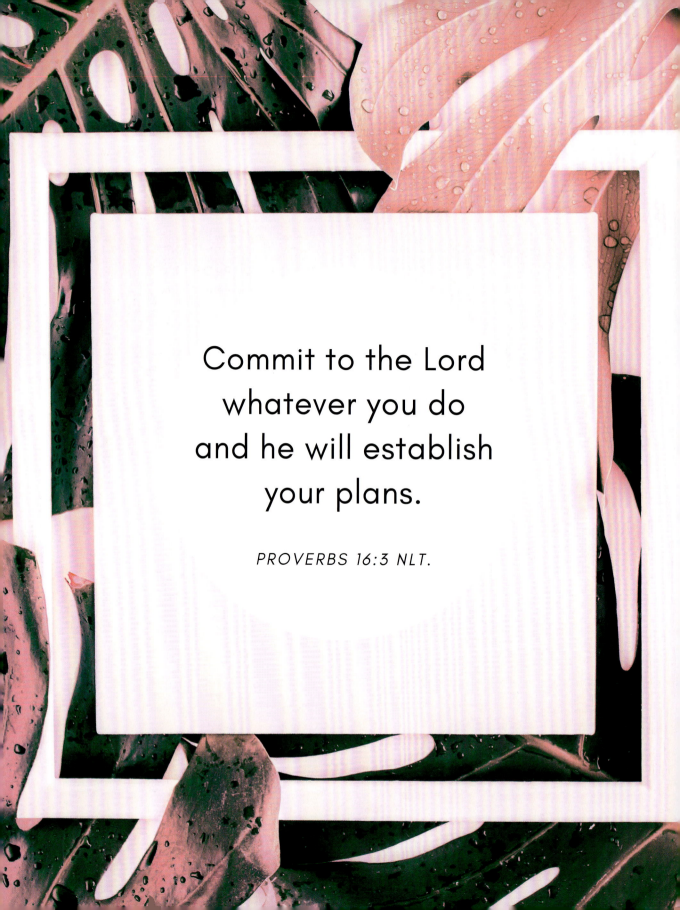

Reflection:

♥ WHAT SITUATION IN YOUR LIFE DO YOU NEED TO LET GO OF? WHICH RELATIONSHIPS/FRIENDSHIPS IS GOD PROMPTING YOU TO RELEASE SO THAT YOU CAN MOVE FORWARD INTO HIS KINGDOM?

_____

_____

_____

_____

_____

_____

_____

Yield!

Romans 12:1-2 NLT.

I appeal to you therefore, brothers and sisters, by the mercies of God, to present your bodies as a living sacrifice, holy and acceptable to God, which is your spiritual worship. Do not be conformed to this world, but be transformed by the renewal of your mind, that by testing you may discern what is the will of God, what is good and accepetable and perfect.

YIELDING TO GOD

Dear God, I have learned that before You can introduce new things, You remove the old and often dismantle the models that no longer serve us. I pray for total surrender to all that You are undoing in my life and yield to all that You are doing. Your plan is perfect. Your will is perfect. Your way is perfect and Your word is perfect. Lord I, _____, (insert name) yield to You. Refine me, Lord, in the furnace of affliction. I declare that the refining and polishing of God is taking place and I will come out as pure gold. Your plan stands firm. Father, today, I thank You for the season of separation. Separate me Lord. Show me another side of Yourself. Cause me to come into a fresh revelation that I will carry into the next season. You have changed the order and I declare that You, Lord, are the God that changes times and seasons. Thank You that even with my present circumstances right now, You are changing times and seasons, because of what You have released in heaven. I pray that You establish me in the realm where You want me to be. Let Your will be done in me and through me. *In Isaiah 55:8, You say that Your thoughts are nothing like our thoughts; Your ways are far beyond anything we could imagine and just as heavens are higher than the earth, so are You ways and thoughts.* I can make many plans but Your purpose will prevail. So Father I ask You to give me Your wisdom and knowledge. I believe and trust that You will go before me, leveling mountains, smashing down gates of bronze and cutting through bars of iron; Make pathways through wilderness and create rivers in the dry wasteland. I give You praise and thanks as You refresh me, for You are doing something new in the world and in each of us. Dear God, I humble myself before You and surrender to that which You have uprooted and torn down. I embrace Your will and declare that it is setting up the course of my life. Clear the way for Your glory. In Jesus' name I pray, Amen.

Reflection:

♥ HAVE I YIELDED ALL AREAS OF MYSELF AND MY LIFE TO GOD? HAVE I YIELDED TO GOD'S WILL FOR MY LIFE? IF NOT, WHAT CAN I DO TO FULLY IMMERSE MYSELF IN HIM?

_____

_____

_____

_____

_____

_____

_____

NEW LIFE

"For you were buried with Christ when you were baptized. And with Him you were raised to new life because you trusted the mighty power of God, who raised Christ from the dead." Colossians 2:12

Dear heavenly Father, I know You have a new life waiting for me and I know things won't change until I change. Thank You for purchasing my freedom and forgiving me of all my sins. Thank You for rescuing me out of the kingdom of darkness and taking me into the light, into the kingdom of Your Son. *1 Thessalonians 5:6 says: " For we are children of the light and of the day; we don't belong to darkness and night."* Help me to change my perspective, my mindset and my behavior, taking my mind off things of the past so I can move forward into Your promises. I want to see things through the eyes of faith, and make decisions based on the promises of God. Lord, as I learn to know You better, make my ways honorable and pleasing unto You. I also pray that You will strengthen me with Your mighty power to have endurance and patience so that I may not be discouraged or lose sight of what You want to accomplish through me. I declare right now, in the mighty name of Jesus, that any sinful, earthly things lurking within me - anger, rage, malicious behavior, slander or dirty language, be put to death. Let my conversations be gracious and my behavior attractive, living in holiness and honor. I strip myself of my old sinful nature and ask God to clothe me with mercy, kindness, humility, gentleness and patience. Above all, I ask the Holy Spirit to clothe me with the love of God and the peace of Christ. Keep me devoted to prayer, reading Your word, praise and worship, and give me the spirit of discernment and understanding. Today, I completely let go of the old and take hold of the new, trusting God to take me through. I will walk all the way through to victory by the grace of God. I am going to be who God designed me to be and do what He willed me to do. In Jesus' name, Amen.

Anyone who belongs to Christ has become a new person. The old life is gone; a new life has begun!

2 CORINTHIANS 5:17 NLT.

Reflection:

♥ WHAT MINDSETS AND BEHAVIORS DO I NEED TO CHANGE TO LIVE A LIFE THAT IS HONORING AND PLEASING UNTO GOD?

_____

_____

_____

_____

_____

_____

_____

Reset

And I will give you a new heart, and I will put a new spirit in you. I will take out your stony, stubborn heart and give you a tender, responsive heart.

EZEKIEL 36:26 NLT.

RESET

Almighty and loving God, today I come before You asking that You reset my mind and heart. I pray You will help me to spend less time thinking and overthinking and more time preaching and reminding myself of Your truth. Your word is enough, Your grace is enough and Your blood is enough for me. Help me to no longer live by my situation but by Your revelation. I know You stand beside me and I know You're in the fire with me. Father of compassion, I pray You will keep me reminded that You dwell within me. I ask that you let the God in me speak continually to me. I pray You will cast out any spirit within me that whispers lies. Cast out any doubt, any fear and any insecurity in my heart and mind. Help me to not be double-minded. Help me to not accept my default attitude towards anything. I pray You will change me from within and let my new beliefs drive my behaviors. Dear God, let the words of my mouth and the meditations of my heart be acceptable and pleasing unto You. Take charge of my heart - guard and guide it. Let my new habits create the condition of my heart. Set my heart and mind in the right direction. I decree and declare a reset of my heart and mind, turning away from the things beneath and setting them on the things above. God, my purifier, let Your call awaken me. Let Your presence continue to grow within me. Instill a new awareness of You and what You desire of me. I decree and declare from this day forward that I love and have the presence of God. I love the Word of God. I love the ways, works and will of God. In the mighty name of Jesus, Amen.

Reflection:

♥ HAVE I GIVEN GOD PERMISSION TO RESET MY HEART AND MIND? WHAT DO I NEED GOD TO CAST OUT OF MY HEART AND MIND?

_____

_____

_____

_____

_____

_____

_____

Clean Heart

Let us go right into the presence of God with sincere hearts fully trusting him. For our guilty conscience have been sprinkled with Christ's blood to make us clean, and our bodies have been washed with pure water.

Hebrew 10:22 nlt.

CLEAN HEART

"If we say we have no sin, we deceive ourselves, and the truth is not in us [but if] we confess our sins, he is faithful and just to forgive us our sins and to cleanse us from all unrighteousness." 1 John 1:9–10

My Amazing Father, Thank You for Your unconditional love. I rejoice in the knowing that You will never stop loving me. Thank You for waking me up to see a new day. Dear Lord, today I thank You for another chance to get things right. Shift me into a new place in You. I let go of old ways of doing and thinking. *Search me, God, and know my heart; test me and know my anxious thoughts. See if there is anything offensive in me, and lead me in the way everlasting. (Psalm 139: 23-24).* Today, God, I give You full access to every room in my heart. I pray You search my heart and show me the things that are not of You. Uproot any and everything that does not belong there, until I look like You on the inside and behave like You on the outside. Cast out any ungodly spirits within me; jealousy and envy, you have to go. Bitterness and resentment, you must leave. Malice and unforgiveness, you cannot stay here. Wash me thoroughly from my iniquity and cleanse me from my sins; ones I have committed knowingly and unknowingly. Save me, Lord, by Your mercy. *Matthew 5:8 says: "Blessed are the pure in heart, for they shall see God."* Help me to recognize You more so that I am filled with Your goodness and to live a life that is obedient and pleasing unto You. Position my heart so that You can shape and refine me into Your image. Dear Father in Heaven, I want more of You and less of me. I pour out all I have and lay down all I am. Fill me with Your spirit and let me overflow. Shine through me, bless others through me and use me for Your greater good. Help me to love like Jesus, to be understanding and forgiving, honest and sincere. Father God, help me to stay reminded of who I am in You, as I try to be the very best version of me. I pray this with a humbled heart, in Jesus' name, Amen.

Reflection:

♥ WHAT DOES GOD WANT TO CLEANSE ME FROM? WHAT WOULD HE LKIE TO UPROOT FROM MY HEART THAT IS NOT OF HIM?

_____

_____

_____

_____

_____

_____

_____

Submit

DO NOT BE STUBBORN, AS THEY WERE, BUT SUBMIT YOURSELVES TO THE LORD. COME TO HIS TEMPLE, WHICH HE HAS SET APART AS HOLY FOREVER. WORSHIP THE LORD YOUR GOD SO THAT HIS FIERCE ANGER WILL TURN AWAY FROM YOU.

2 Chronicles 30:8 nlt.

SUBMIT UNTO GOD

Dear Heavenly and Righteous Father, I know that I can't stay where I am, stuck in this world. I have a burning desire to move forward in You. Obedience requires me to humble myself and surrender to Your authority. So, Lord, today I humble myself before Thee and choose right now to obey You, subject and submit myself completely to You. I say YES to Your will and choose to move forward in Your purpose and plans; not according to my old way of life. I rebuke any spirit that is keeping me from obeying You, In the name of Jesus Christ and I ask that You continue to guide my path and protect me on this journey. Help me to stay my course, to not swerve to the left or to the right, as I remain fixated on You. Dear God, I ask for Your peace and happiness on this path, and courage to face any obstacle I may come across. I ask for Your strength to press forward wisely. *Romans 8:28 says, "And we know that all things work together for good to those who love God, to those who are called according to His purpose."* So, God I pray and trust that all things are working together for my greater good and that I can have faith knowing that Your will is the greatest will. I accept Your grace and provision to walk in Your Spirit. Provide a change in my heart and in my mind. I pray that my heart's desires be aligned with the will of God, letting the glory be unto You. I thank You, Lord, that You are my Shepherd and I will not want for anything; that in You, I have everything I need to thrive. Help me to trust Your leading. Thank You for ministering strength to my spiritual, emotional, physical and financial needs. As I submit to You, every area of my life is being made strong. Thank You for Your blessings of peace, and the gift of grace that I gain from humbly surrendering myself to You, as nothing in this world could ever compare. I trust You. I love You and my faith is in You. Amen.

Reflection:

♥ WHICH AREA OF MY LIFE DO I NEED TO SUBMIT UNTO GOD?

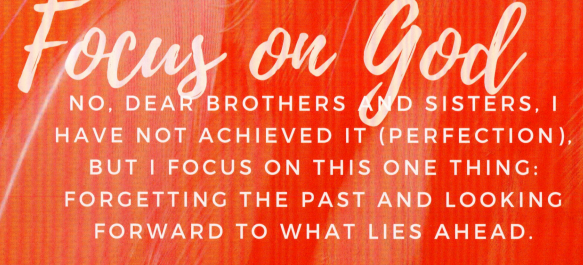

Focus on God

NO, DEAR BROTHERS AND SISTERS, I HAVE NOT ACHIEVED IT (PERFECTION), BUT I FOCUS ON THIS ONE THING: FORGETTING THE PAST AND LOOKING FORWARD TO WHAT LIES AHEAD.

Philippians 3:13 nlt.

FOCUS ON GOD

"Blessed are the meek, for they will inherit the earth, blessed are those who hunger and thirst for righteousness, for they will be filled, blessed are the merciful, for they will be shown mercy, blessed are the pure in heart, for they will see God. Blessed are the peacemakers, for they will be called sons of God." Matthew 5: 5-9

Dear God, You are my loving Father, with whom I desire to have a strong and meaningful relationship. You speak to us in so many ways, so Lord, I pray today that You will open my eyes to see Your truth; to open my ears to hear You with clarity and open my heart to receive You fully. Speak to me through Your word, through Your Holy Spirit and from the depth of my heart. I need You, heavenly Father. I need Your wisdom and guidance but, most importantly, I need Your will to be done in every part of my life. Help me to fix my eyes on You. Help me to fix my eyes on the unseen as the things I can see are temporary. I know You are eager to bless me but God I pray that You will help me, not to seek blessings, but rather, to seek the source of these blessings. For as Your Word says, *"Seek first the kingdom of God and his righteousness, and all these things will be added to you." (Matthew 6:33).* Almighty Father, help me to use Your word as a mirror, to continually check myself for shortcomings. Help me not to measure myself against others but to measure myself to God's perfection. Help me to listen, more carefully, to what You are saying to me. While the world is saying and offering so many things, keep me reminded that You are the way, the truth and the life. Lord, right now, I declare over my life that I will not be swayed by the world's glittery distractions but stay committed unto You. Crucify my flesh with its passions and desires and lead me into the path of righteousness. Grant me the courage to stand for the love of Christ and let people see You in me. Let my life represent who and what I stand for. Let me demonstrate the qualities of a godly person - love, forgiveness, peace, joy, humility, gentleness and self- control - and let me become and act like what I truly believe in. In Your precious and holy name, Amen.

Reflection

♥ WHAT AM I FOCUSED ON? AM I FOCUSED ON MY PROBLEMS OR ON THE THINGS ABOVE? WHAT STEPS CAN I TAKE TO REDIRECT MY FOCUS?

_____

_____

_____

_____

_____

_____

_____

Time
DEVOTE YOURSELVES TO PRAYER WITH AN ALERT MIND AND A THANKFUL HEART.

Colossians 4:2 NLT

TIME

"If you look for me wholeheartedly, you will find me." Jeremiah 29:13

Dear Heavenly Father, Great is Thy Faithfulness. I am so grateful for my relationship with You. You are so loving, so understanding, forgiving, kind and merciful to me. Lord as I embark on this journey with You, I pray You give me the desire to want to spend time with You, to want to get to know You as much as You know me. Give me the hunger and thirst for the filling of Your word. I know God that spending time with You will not only fix my problems but will increase my happiness and peace beyond understanding, give me wholeness, boldness and confidence, change my image and bring me deliverance. Only with You am I satisfied and content in this world, only with You I am victorious and courageous. I want to seek You diligently and wholeheartedly because only in Your presence will I find the fullness of joy. I can only stay strong when I stay in You. I pray for the discipline to give You the first portion of each day so that the rest of it may be blessed. And as I spend more time with You, I ask that things will change radically in my life. Go to war on my behalf, intercede on my behalf, soften hearts and open doors on my behalf. The more I put in You, Lord, I pray the more you will pour out of me. God, I pray as I delve into your word that I will enjoy You, learn to behold You and just continue to be amazed by Your presence. Let Your words settle in my heart and when I need them most bring them out of me. When I feel weak, weary or heavy, remind me to put on the garment of praise, and worship You in every situation and circumstance. As I abide in You, so shall You abide in me. In the name of Your Son, Jesus Christ, Amen.

So humble yourselves under the almighty power of God, & at the right time he will lift you up in honor.

1 PETER 5:6 NLT

Reflection:

♥ HAVE I PRIORITISED SPENDING TIME WITH GOD? IF NOT, HOW I CAN I SPEND MORE QUALITY TIME WITH HIM? (READING THE WORD, PRAYING).

Faith

Then Jesus told them, "I tell you the truth, if you have faith and don't doubt, you can do things like this and much more. You can even say to this mountain, " May you be lifted up and thrown into the sea," and it will happen.

Matthew 21:21 NLT

WALKING IN FAITH

"Then Jesus said to the disciples, " Have faith in God. I tell you the truth, you can say to this mountain, "May you be lifted up and thrown into the sea," and it will happen. But you must really believe it will happen and have no doubt in your heart. I tell you, you can pray for anything and if you believe that you've received it, it will be yours." Mark 11: 22-24

Dear heavenly Father, how great is Your faithfulness! Thank You for being faithful to me even when I murmur and complain. Thank You for being faithful to me even when I turn from You. Dear God, thank You for being faithful even when I know Your will is best for my life but I make it so difficult to move forward in and with You. Lord, I know walking in faith is the only way I can remain resting in You. Help me to be more than just a believer; let my faith activate the unseen. Teach me how to be seeded in You, Christ Jesus, standing in faith and standing against the enemy. Show me how to operate in faith, declaring and demanding victory, speaking Your words with power and authority, re-aligning myself with You. Help me to simply trust You as You magnify Yourself in my life. Let me hear Your word, believe Your word and accept Your word, speaking them through the words of my mouth and the works of my hands. Dear God, I know that without faith it is impossible to please You. So I pray You will grant me radical faith and the patience to wait for You to act and the strength to continuously declare the outcome. Give me the courage to start where I am, working up to where You want me to be, knowing that You will direct and redirect every time. Give me the kind of faith that does not accept no for an answer. Position me, Lord, to receive Your blessings as I earnestly listen for each of Your commands. In the name of Jesus Christ, Amen.

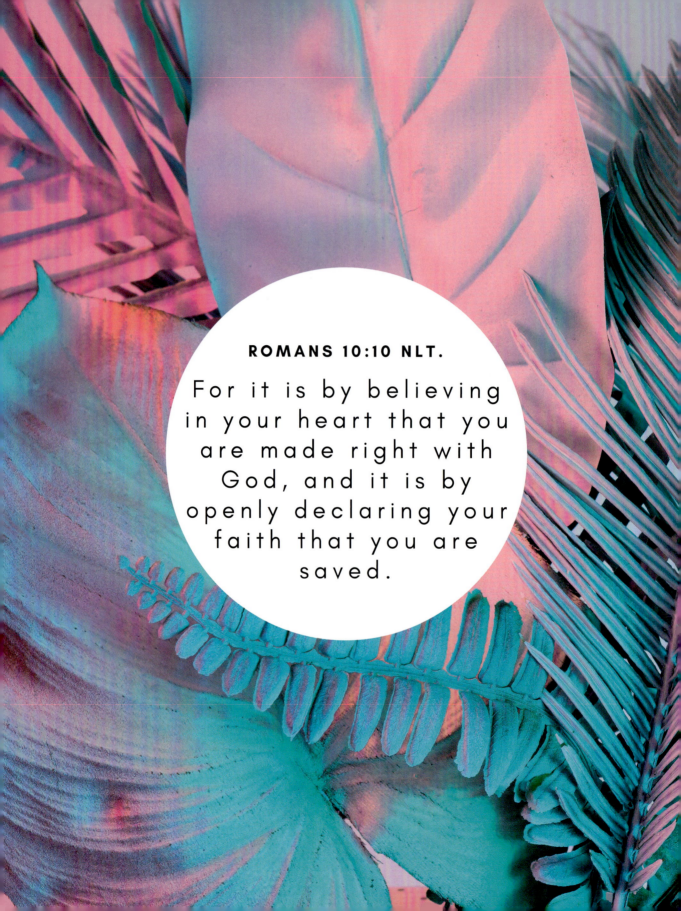

Reflection:

♥ AM I WALKING IN FEAR OR FAITH? HOW CAN I BECOME MORE FAITHFUL IN GOD? WHAT CAN I DO TO GROW MY FAITH IN HIM?

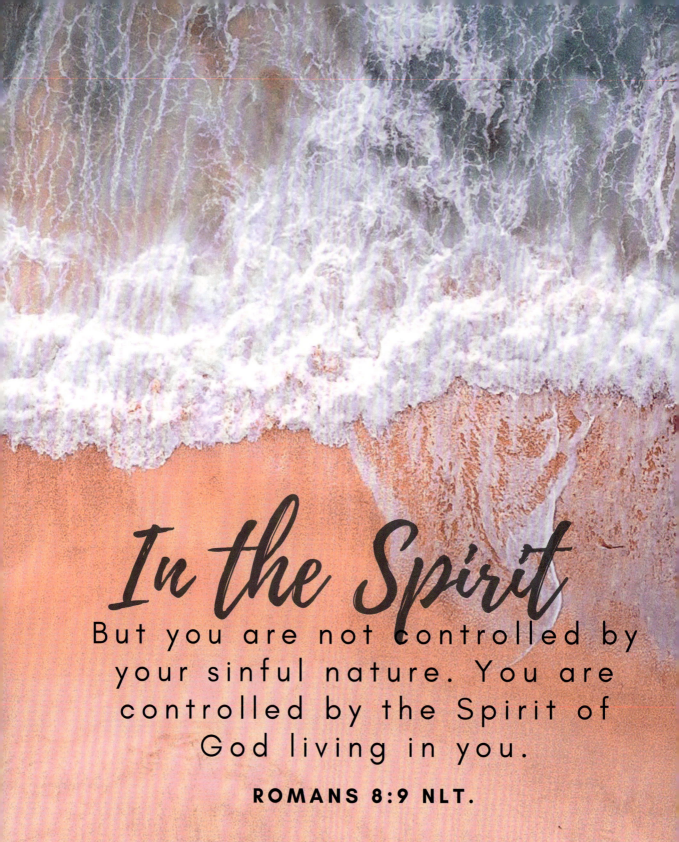

In the Spirit

But you are not controlled by your sinful nature. You are controlled by the Spirit of God living in you.

ROMANS 8:9 NLT.

LIVING IN THE SPIRIT

Dear Father in heaven, I come before You today asking for Your help and guidance to live in the Spirit. I pray that You help me to develop and be built up spiritually and to give me the indispensable quality to be sensitive to Your spirit. Give me the discipline to make time for Your word, the discernment and wisdom when meditating on the word and the desire to do according to all that is written. Get rid of any unbelief within me, God, and give me the confidence to think and speak with certainty. Grant me the courage to be a doer of the new covenant, walking by faith. As of today, I will give the word of God first place in my life, inclining my ears unto what it is saying, letting it not depart from my eyes and keeping it in the midst of my heart, for it is life unto those who find it. As I do this, I believe and trust that You will make my way prosperous and successful. Strengthen the voice of my spirit and give me the obedience to listen as the Holy Spirit dwells within me. As your word says, in Proverbs 20:27, *The spirit of man is a candle of the Lord.* Sharpen my spiritual senses and let me not be oblivious to the things of the unseen world. As I stay connected to You in prayer and the reading of Your word, let me feel Your presence in my constant walk with You. In Jesus' name I pray, Amen.

Since we are living by the Spirit, let us follow the Spirit's leading in every part of our lives

Galations 5:15.

Reflection:

♥ IS THE HOLY SPIRIT DWELLING WITHIN ME? AM I LIVING IN THE SPIRIT OR IN THE FLESH? WHAT CAN I DO TO BECOME MORE OF HIM AND LESS OF ME?

_____

_____

_____

_____

_____

_____

_____

Grace

Each time he said, "My grace is all you need. My power works best in weakness." So now I am glad to boast about my weakness, so that the power of Christ can work through me.

2 CORINTHIANS 12:9 NLT

GRACE TO EMBRACE

God of all love and all grace, I come before You, today, thanking You for everything You continue to do in and around me. Thank You for every season of life. Help me to embrace the things that make me different, for these are the things that will drive me to my destiny. Help me to love the things about myself that embarrasses me the most, for these are the very things You will use to empower me to make a difference in Your Kingdom. Dear God, help me not to run from the things You wish to use to lead me into my greatest season. You have spoken over my life. Your word says in *2 Corinthians 5:17 - "Therefore, if anyone is in Christ, the new creation has come: The old has gone, the new is here!"* Separate me from people and circumstances and propel me into my calling. Show me how to be distinctive. Give me the characteristics of a child of God and distinguish me from the world. Help me to not run back to what is familiar or trade in special for similar. Get the greatest glory out of my life as I continuously change for the better. Teach me how to be a perfect follower of Your Kingdom and leader in this world. Teach me how to bear spiritual fruit as I abide in You. Teach me obedience, righteousness and godliness. Give me the willingness to obey and do Your will and Your grace to not wilfully or habitually sin. Bestow upon me the discipline to do what is deemed right by You, Lord. I pray You will lead me by Your Spirit, guide me into all the truth and put to death the deeds of my flesh. In Your Heavenly Name I pray, Amen.

Reflection:

♥ IS THERE ANYTHING ABOUT MYSELF THAT I NEED'S GOD GRACE TO HELP ME ACCEPT? WHAT HAS GOD'S GRACE SAVED ME FROM? DO I NEED GOD'S GRACE TO SAVE ME FROM SOMETHING?

COURAGE

"So be strong and courageous! Do not be afraid and do not panic before them. For the Lord your God will personally go ahead of you. He will neither fail you nor abandon you." Deuteronomy 31:6

My gracious Father, Your word commands us to be strong and courageous, not frightened or dismayed. Today I pray for the courage to be free to be who I am in You. Give me a kind of confidence that strengthens and sustains me. Dear God, it is foolish of me to live an unfulfilling life, trying to impress people or to be like anyone else. Keep me reminded, Lord God, that You are the standard, for only Your ways are perfect and pure. I know on this path I have chosen, many people will judge, misunderstand, reject and persecute me, but grant me the courage to stay on course. *In Romans 8:31, it says "What shall we then say to these things? If God be for us, who can be against us?"* Today, I refuse what's going on in the world. I refuse to bow down to or to worship carnal things. Give me the courage and grace to want to please You and prepare me to handle and persevere in the face of adversity. Convict me, correct me and redirect my life. Change the way I see myself and change how others see me. Help me to be obedient and willing to do Your work. Even when people may belittle or shun me, remind me of who I am in You and that my value is who I am in Christ. Help me to stand up for what is right and help me to face suffering with dignity and faith. Help me to not compromise who I am or what God wants me to do; to see beyond present trials and face the future with confidence. Give me satisfaction in Your favor and let Your light shine through me to glorify my Father in heaven. So that I may be a shining example for others to follow, in Jesus' name, Amen.

SO TAKE COURAGE!

FOR I BELIEVE GOD. IT WILL BE JUST AS HE SAID.

Acts 27:25 NLT.

Reflection:

♥ WHAT DO I NEED MORE COURAGE TO DO? WHAT DO I NEED MORE COURAGE TO WALK AWAY FROM OR WALK INTO?

Love

Dear friends, let us continue to love one another, for love comes from God. Anyone who loves is a child of God. But anyone who does not love does not know God, for God is love.

1 JOHN 4:7-8 NLT.

LOVE

"You must love the Lord your God with all your heart, all your soul, and all your mind. This is the first and greatest commandment. A second is equally important: Love your neighbor as yourself." Matthew 22:37 – 39

My amazing and righteous Father, I love You so much. Thank You for being all that You are. Thank You for being so relentless, so marvelous and so gracious. I am humbled by Your love. Thank You for loving me like no other, always forgiving and always finding a way back to my heart. What would I be without You? I was lost and You found me. I was blind and You made me see. Thank You for embracing me personally and intimately, never leaving or forsaking me. Let there be no distance between us, keep drawing me closer to Your heart. Dear God, as You have loved me, help me to love others. Help me to love the unlovable with the love of Jesus Christ. For Your word says in *Matthew 5:47 "For if you love those who love you, what reward can you have?"* Help me to love when no one is watching and when there is nothing in it for me. Give me the desire and the discipline to make time to love, the courage to put aside my pride for love and a heart to always choose love. Help me to represent Christ - having a Godly character and walking in the fruit of the Spirit. My flesh is selfish and self-centred. Help me, to not live for me but, to forget myself in order to make others happy. Keep me reminded that it is not my job to judge or convict but to simply love. I want to make an incredible difference in the lives of others, adding value to those who cross my path. Make me a blessing dear God, and let others see You through me. Help me to always, always remember : *Love is patient, love is kind. It does not envy, it does not boast, it is not proud. It does not dishonor others, it is not self-seeking, it is not easily angered, it keeps no record of wrongs. Love does not delight in evil but rejoices with the truth. It always protects, always trusts, always hopes, always perseveres. Love never fails. (1 Corinthians 13: 4-8). In Jesus's name,* Amen.

Reflection:

♥ IS THERE ANYONE IN MY LIFE THAT I DEEM HARD TO LOVE? IS THERE ANYONE I COULD SHOW MORE/SOME LOVE TO? HOW CAN I BE MORE LOVING?

1 Corinthians 13:13 : Three things will last forever - faith, hope and love - and the greatest of these is love.

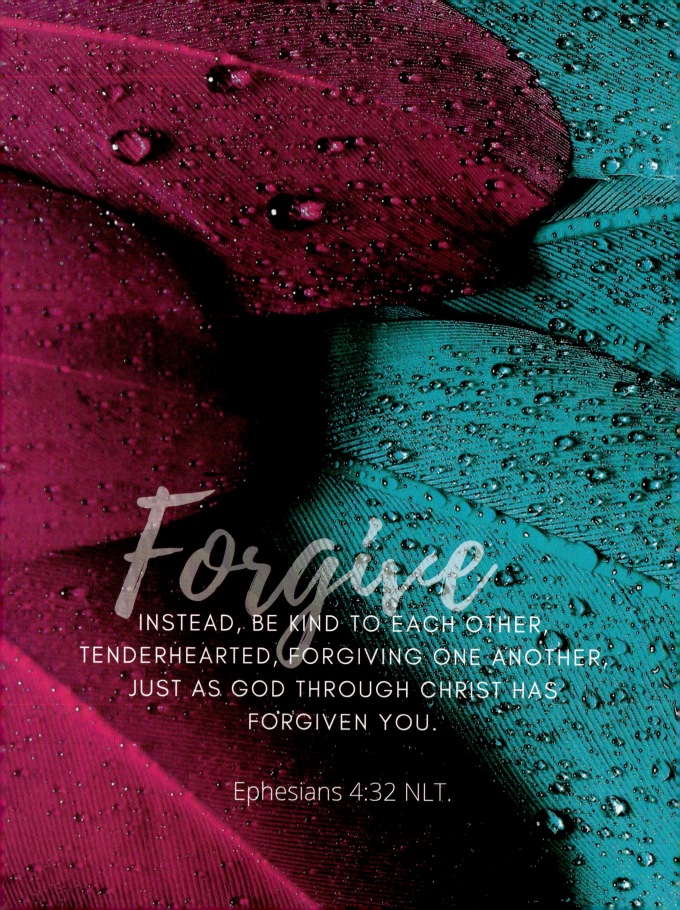

FORGIVENESS

"Bless those who curse you. Pray for those who hurt you." Luke 6:28

Dear Merciful Father, Thank You for Your wisdom that teaches me how to live an upright and pleasing life unto You. God of mercy and compassion, I ask for Your forgiveness and freedom from all consequences of my sins. Dear God, they say "sticks and stones may break my bones but words can never harm me," but this, Lord, I have found to be so untrue. A lot of pain in my life was caused by people around me, their thoughts of me and their words against me, but the devil is a liar and he came to kill, steal and destroy. Kill my beliefs, steal my joy and destroy my faith but God I know You are the way the truth and the life and just as You have loved me, forgiven me countless times, been patient with me and never left my side, I pray you give me the mercy to treat my enemies the same. Today, I consciously decide to release feelings of resentment or vengeance toward anyone who has hurt me. I pray You remove any spirit of unforgiveness or bitterness from my heart today, Lord. I pray You will grant me Your peace beyond understanding and the truth of Your spirit to always know who I am in You. Help me to not let the behavior of others compromise who I am. Help me to be like Jesus, to always represent His character. He did not change when He was betrayed, denied, judged, criticized or rejected. When I am really hurt, help me to walk in love, declaring blessings and happiness for those who have wronged me. I trust that You will take care of it and I believe in You to work it out for good. Let me bring peace wherever I go, not allowing people to make me unhappy. Keep me reminded that only hurt people, hurt people. So, instead of letting my feelings distract me from what I am called to do, remind me that I am a source of love and joy to others. *Romans 12:21 says "Don't let evil conquer you, but conquer evil by doing good."*

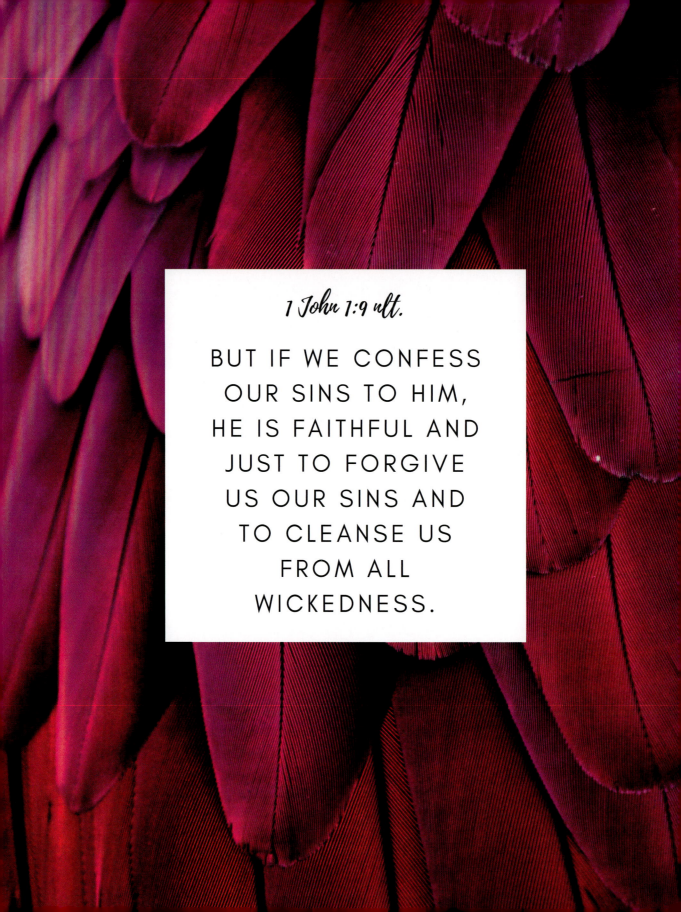

Reflection:

♥ WHO HAS CAUSED ME HURT/ANGER OR DISAPPOINTMENT? WHO DO I NEED TO FORGIVE AND RELEASE TO GOD TODAY?

_____

_____

_____

_____

_____

In the mighty name of Jesus, I forgive _____, for any pain they caused upon my life. I pray they will come to know you and I pray that they will find peace and happiness in you by the grace of God. I pray that whatever pain they are feeling, that You God will intervene on their behalf and shine your face upon their life. I release them from my heart in the name of Jesus Christ and pray you fill it with love, joy and understanding in Jesus' name I pray, Amen.

Discipline

THINK ABOUT IT: JUST AS A PARENT DISCIPLINES A CHILD, THE LORD YOUR GOD DISCIPLINES YOU FOR YOUR OWN GOOD.

Deuteronomy 8:5 NLT

DISCIPLINE

"Whoever loves instruction loves knowledge, But he who hates correction is stupid." Proverbs 12:1

My loving God, Today, I thank You for Your love for me. I thank You that You are my provider, my comforter, my friend and my father. As my Father, I know You only want the best for me and in wanting the best for me, You sometimes have to discipline me. Today, God, I pray that when I steer in the wrong direction and mess up, You will keep me reminded that Your discipline is merely an expression of Your great love for me and that there is no condemnation for those in Christ. I come before You praying and asking that You will drive all bad habits out of me. I ask for Your help so that the devil cannot reign and captivate my body, mind or spirit. I pray that You will give me the discipline to walk in the spirit, not fulfilling the lust of my flesh. Help me to look away from all that distracts me from walking in Your truth. Dear Jesus, I call upon Your blessed name, asking that You will break any harmful habits out of my life. In Your power, I pray You will deliver me from anger, bitterness, self pity, sexual immorality, depression or any other habit that separates me from You. Help me to not be quick tempered, impulsive or or easily offended. I pray that I will have the discipline to manage my emotions and behavior, not allowing them to manage me. Help me to focus on forming new habits that are pleasing unto You. As I earnestly seek You, let the peace of God rule as an umpire in my life. Let the fruits of His Spirit - peace, love, gentleness, self-control, joy, kindness, goodness, faithfulness and patience - guide me. In Your name I pray, Amen.

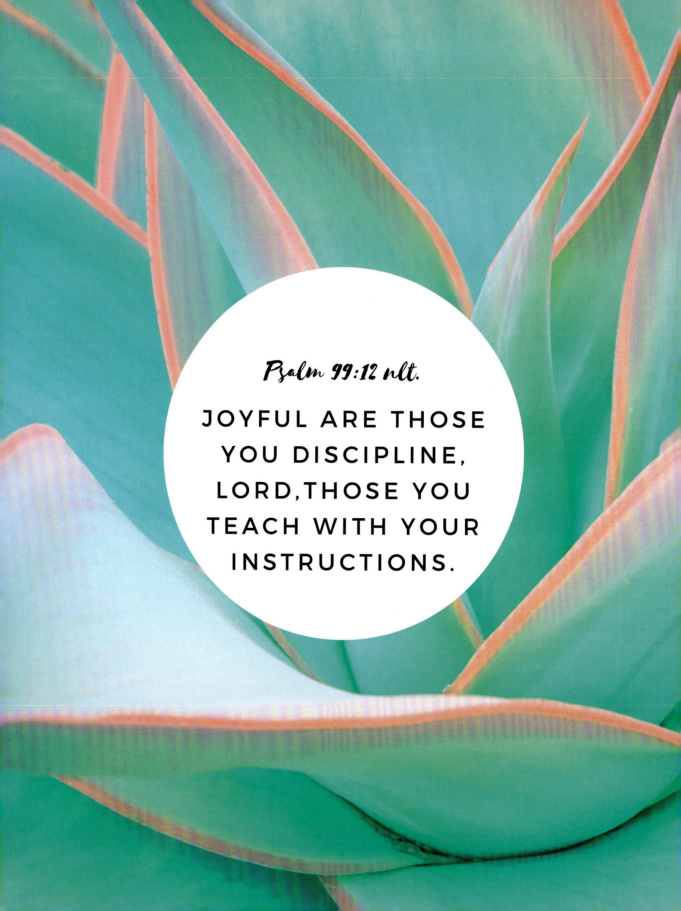

Psalm 94:12 nlt.

JOYFUL ARE THOSE YOU DISCIPLINE, LORD, THOSE YOU TEACH WITH YOUR INSTRUCTIONS.

Reflection:

♥ WHICH AREAS OF MY LIFE DO I NEED TO APPLY MORE DISCIPLINE IN? HOW CAN I EXERCISE MORE DISCIPLINE IN THESE AREAS?

_____

_____

_____

_____

_____

_____

_____

Trust

I PRAY THAT GOD, THE SOURCE OF HOPE, WILL FILL YOU COMPLETELY WITH JOY AND PEACE BECAUSE YOU TRUST HIM. THEN YOU WILL OVERFLOW WITH CONFIDENT HOPE THROUGH THE POWER OF THE HOLY SPIRIT.

Romans 15:13 nlt.

TRUST

Dear God, thank You for being a God of promises. Thank You that Your word never comes back void and thank You that You work things for good for those that love You and are called according to Your purpose. Dear God, today, I pray for the firm belief in Your reliability and truth. Help me to simply believe that You love me, You are good, You have the power and are willing to help me. Teach me, God, to not just trust You for something but to trust You through things, even when I don't understand or when You are not giving me what I want. 1 Corinthians 13:9 states that " *Our knowledge is partial and incomplete, and even the gift of prophecy reveals only part of the whole picture.*" Help me to trust in Your perfect timing, that You will reveal things when the time is right. Help me to trust You when everything is shaking and my world seems to be falling apart. Let me not place my confidence in myself or others, to not rely on my own capacity to figure things out but to know You will take care of it. Psalm 37:3 says to trust in the Lord and do good. Dear God, while I trust and wait on You, show me how to sow good seeds, give me the kindness and love to help others even when I cannot help myself. Show me how to trust You and enjoy life while You are solving my problems. Dear God, I want to be amazed by Your mysteries, amazed by Your wonders and power. Trusting You is a decision, so from here on I choose to trust in Your love and goodness and I trust that I have an expected end. You are my strength and stronghold and I take refuge in You. In Jesus' name I pray, Amen.

>

PHILLIPIANS 4:6 NLT

Don't worry about anything; instead, pray about everything.

Tell God what you need, and thank Him for all He has done.

Reflection:

♥ AM I TRUSTING IN MY OWN ABILITIES OR IN GOD? WHAT AREAS IN MY LIFE DO I NEED TO TRUST GOD MORE WITH?

Confidence

But let us who live in the light be clearheaded, protected by the armor of faith and love, and wearing as our helmet the confidence of our salvation.

1 THESSALONIANS 5:8 NLT

CONFIDENCE

Dear merciful Father, Thank You for this day; another day to witness Your goodness and grace. Dear God, sometimes I struggle with having confidence in both You and myself. I know You love me with an everlasting love but sometimes I find it hard to apply that knowledge during trials and tribulations. I know You are a God of power and strength as You have proven this again and again both in Your word and in my life.. During times of hardships, please help me to ignore feelings of doubt and uncertainty and go with what I know to be true. Keep me reminded that I can be confident in You. You are for me, You are with me and you are always on my side. Help me to build my confidence not in myself or in flesh but in You. Help me not to display confidence in my own abilities, knowing well that if it is Your will, You will enable me. Let worries and fear never steal my attention. Cause me to remember each and every time You have rescued me leaving me in awe at Your miraculous works. I know that real confidence is having faith in You. I ask that You will activate my faith, dear Jesus, and give me the gifts needed to accomplish the things required of me. Only with You can I step out in faith, only with You can I step against fear; only when I am confident in You can I take action even when I am terrified. Help me to have a positive attitude about what I can do and not worry about all the things I can't do as Your strength is made perfect in my weakness. I refuse to look back, I refuse to be negative, I refuse to be pitiful. Instead, I will be confident, I will look forward, I will have a positive attitude and I will be powerful. In the mighty name of Jesus Christ, Amen.

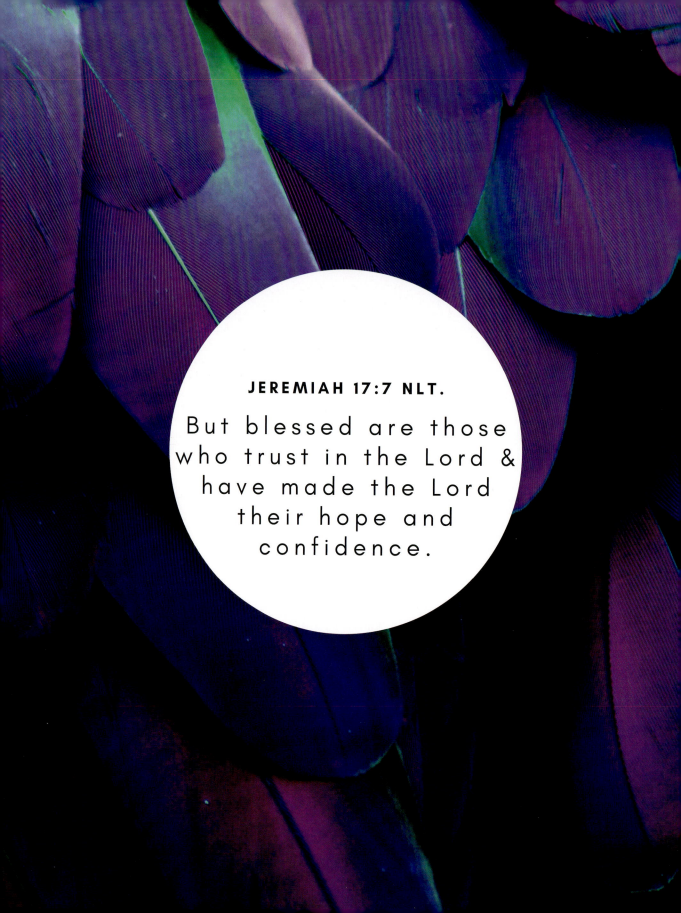

Reflection:

♥ DO I HAVE THE UTMOST CONFIDENCE IN GOD? DO I TRULY BELIEVE HE IS ALL HE SAYS HE IS AND HE IS WILLING AND ABLE TO DO ALL HE SAYS HE WILL DO ? HOW CAN I STRENGTHEN MY CONFIDENCE IN HIM?

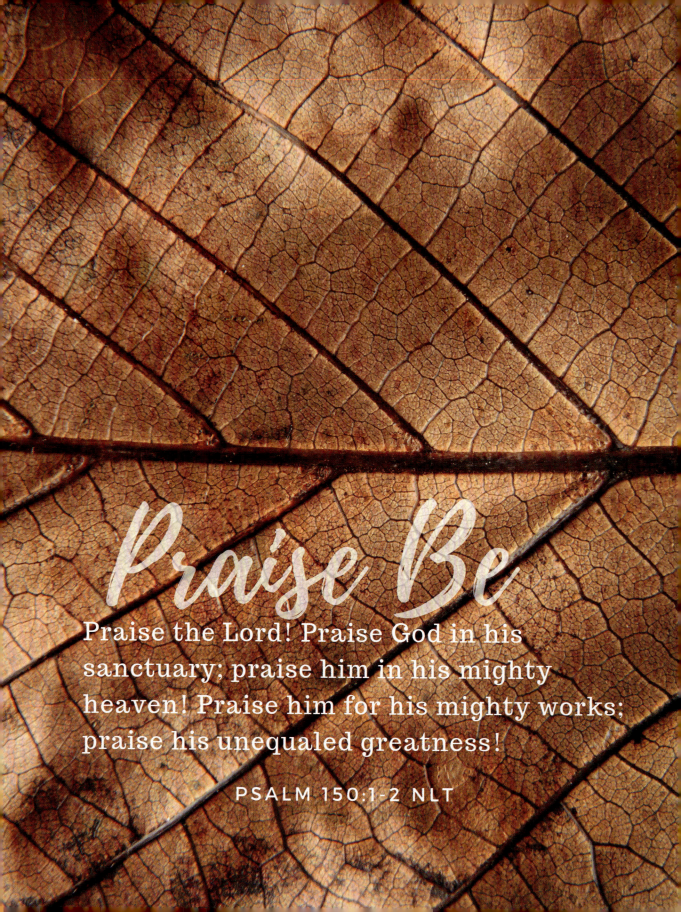

PRAISE BE

You are my God, and I will praise You; You are my God, I will exalt You. Oh, give thanks to the Lord, for He is good! For His mercy endures forever. Psalm 118:28-29

My Living God, Today, I want to praise Your Holy Name. Today, I want to lift Your name on high and give all glory to You. I praise You for all that You are, all that You have done and for all that You continue to do. You are deserving of my praise. My hallelujah belong to You. Today, I express my happiness and gratitude for Your Son, Jesus Christ, who gave His life for me, for my sins and for my freedom. You are my creator. You are my shepherd, my salvation, my comforter, my friend and my father. You have loved me, guided me, protected me and given me Your peace. I am eternally grateful for Your unending mercy, forgiveness and grace. Dear God, let my perpetual praise provide a clear and unhindered passage to You. Sometimes a life of praise is not the easiest or most enjoyable way to live but in my lowest of lows, keep me reminded that it is the most powerful way to change my life. My faith isn't complete without praise. Guide me to praise You in the most uncertain, difficult, frustrating and darkest times. Let my praise to You touch everything and every part of my life. Teach me to praise You not only when things are going my way or when I am in a good mood but also when I feel like my life is out of control, when I don't feel like it. Give me the discipline and desire to rejoice in You always. I accept my responsibility as I am created in Your image and I choose to give thanks and rejoice in You, Lord. Let my praise be a driving force in my life, putting my focus where it needs to be. I will enter Your gates with thanksgiving and a grateful heart. In Jesus' name I pray, Amen.

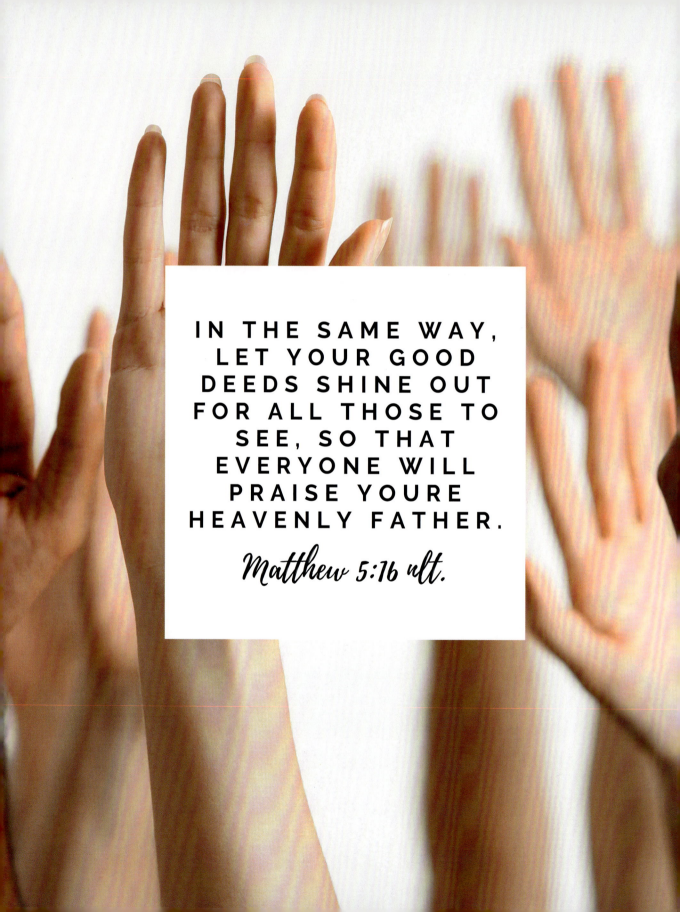

Reflection:

♥ DO I GIVE GOD, PEOPLE OR MYSELF PRAISE? WHAT AM I PRAISING GOD FOR TODAY?

Calling

Look up into the heavens, who created all the stars? He brings them out like an army, one after another, calling each by its name. Because of his great power and incomparable strength, not a single one is missing.

ISAIAH 40:26

CALLING

Dear God, Sometimes I get confused trying to figure out what my calling is. I'm always trying to find that thing that's burning inside of me. Dear God, often I tell myself there has to be more to life than all this temporary happiness because everything else seems so unsatisfying and unfulfilling. I know You are a God of wonders and mystery and even if I missed it the first time, there will be a second because what You have for me will be for me. As I wait for Your perfect timing, help me to continue to develop an intimate relationship with You, honoring, treasuring and valuing You, as You are not just a God of resources. I hearken and make time to hear Your voice as I seek Your revealed will. Help me to not get frustrated with the process or go searching for my purpose but to rest in You, knowing my calling will find me. Help me to know and walk in the truth of You and to not complain or worry over insignificant things. Help me to surround myself with people who bring out the God in me and who will always point me back to the only One who has real power. Give me the wisdom to know and serve the purpose of the season I am in. As I make myself available to You, let Your word become abundant. Rightfully position and equip me to speak for and on behalf of You. As Your word says in 1 John 4:4, *"Greater is He that is in me than he that is in the world."* Fill me with Your spirit and give me all the gifts of the spirit You want me to have so I may serve You in a powerful way. In the name of Jesus Christ, Amen.

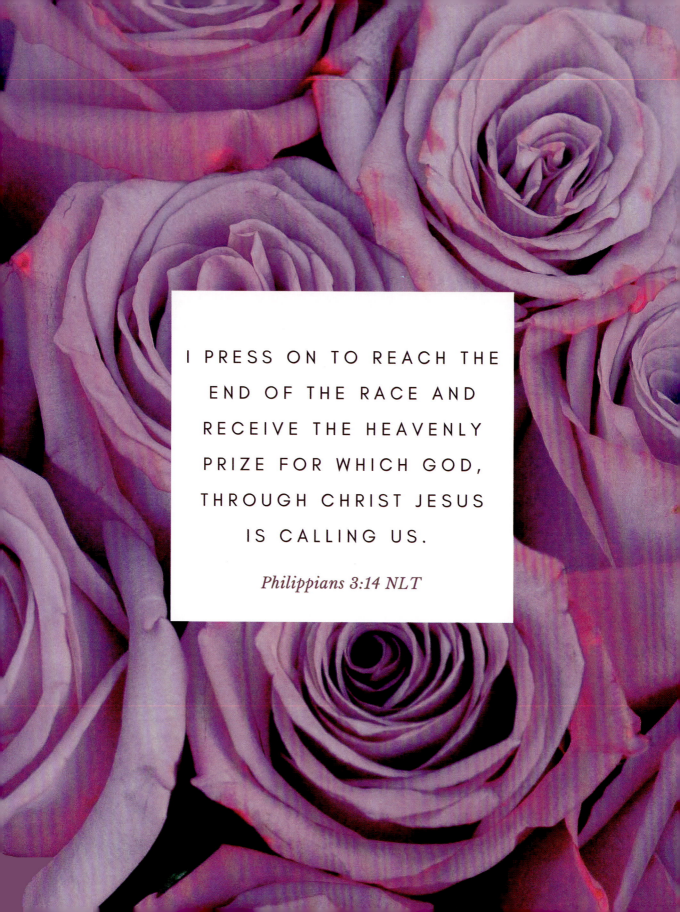

Reflection:

♥ WHAT IS GOD CALLING ME TO DO? AM I WALKING IN MY CALLING?

Higher Purpose

They will be my people, and I will be their God. And I will give them one heart and one purpose: to worship me forever, for their own good and for the good of all their descendants.

JEREMIAH 32:38-39 NLT.

HIGHER PURPOSE

"And we know that God causes everything to work together for the good of those who love Him and are called according to His purpose for them."Romans 8:28

Dear heavenly and righteous Father, Today I bow down before You in humility. Take away from me any spirit of pride, arrogance and boastfulness. Fill me with meekness, submission and modesty. Provide a transformation of my mind and heart today, Lord. Help me to love like Jesus, to pray like Jesus, to walk and talk like Jesus. Do in me what You have been desiring to do and help me to stay the course. God of all things, I gladly accept You even when it is not easy. Fill me completely and fulfill every area of my life. You chose me God, over and over again, so my loving Father, today I choose You and continue to choose You from this day forward. I give myself completely to You. Use me for Your greater good. I do not wish to be half in, half out, but fully immersed in Your kingdom. Obliterate all things not of You and seal shut any door that does not lead to You. I pour out all I have to make room for You. Fill me with the essence of who You are. Continue to be the light in my life and I pray for Your protection as I walk this path. As the mountains around Jerusalem, so surround me, from this time forth and forevermore. Father, any darkness around me - scatter it. Reveal and eradicate everything from my life that is distracting me from walking in my purpose. Dear God, I pray for the presence and infilling of the Holy Spirit. I pray for Your power to fight the things of the unseen world that try to sway me. Help me to walk away from and forget the things of my old path so that I may walk into the higher purpose You have planned for me. I trust in You, dear God, to take away everything from me that represents earth and dust. I do not know where You are taking me but I know You are making me like You and that my old ways are being washed away. Dear Lord, I pray that You use me in a mighty way. No turning back now, I am Yours and You are mine. Show me Your way. In Jesus' name I pray, Amen.

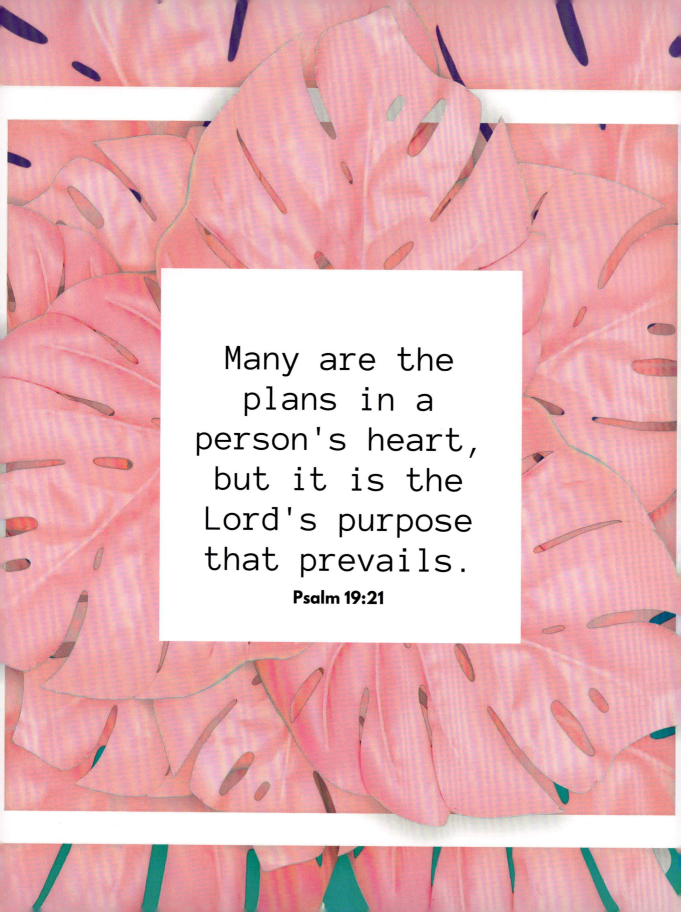

Many are the plans in a person's heart, but it is the Lord's purpose that prevails.

Psalm 19:21

Reflection:

♥ WHAT STEPS DO I NEED TO TAKE TO WALK INTO THE PURPOSE GOD HAS PLANNED FOR ME?

_____

_____

_____

_____

_____

_____

_____

Be Still

Be still before the Lord and wait patiently for him; fret not yourself over the one who prospers in his way, over the man who carries out evil devices.

PSALM 37:7 NLT.

BE STILL

Dear Loving Father, Thank You for not holding my past against me and thank You for making all things new. Thank You for wanting me to live my life to the fullest, fulfilling my passion and purpose in You. Dear God, I cannot enjoy this life and be fearful at the same time. You did not give me a spirit of fear nor did I receive Your Holy Spirit to be fearful. It is impossible for me to believe in the trueness of Jesus Christ and live a life of worry and doubt. So, in the name of Jesus, I cast out any spirit of fear and insecurity; I cast out any spirit of cowardness and consternation and I pray that You replace them with Your power, strength, boldness and authority. For if You are for me who can be against me? You are beside me, before me, behind me and within me. With You I cannot fail. Who cares if the world rejects me when I am already chosen by You? Help me to build a strong foundation with You, Lord Jesus, knowing that when I am loved by You, I can step out and do great things. Dear God, when I am fearful, confused, in turmoil or frustrated, remind me to be still and know that You are God. I declare today that I will not fear failure; I will not fear rejection; I will not fear bad news or trouble because I am God's greatly beloved. You have ordered my steps, and even when I don't understand, I will be confident and determined to stand my ground, knowing that, in God, I have an expected end. You make all things possible and Your word never comes back void. Thank You for being completely trustworthy and faithful. You are the same yesterday, today and tomorrow. Amen.

Reflection:

♥ ARE YOU TRUSTING IN GOD? ARE YOU BEING STILL AND ALLOWING HIM TO BE GOD? WHAT AREA OF YOUR LIFE DO YOU NEED TO BE STILL IN AND ALLOW HIM TO WORK OUT HIS PLAN FOR YOU?

Guidance

My children, listen when your Father corrects you. Pay attention & learn good judgement, for I am giving you good guidance.

Proverbs 4:1 NLT.

GUIDANCE

"Whether you turn to the right or to the left, your ears will hear a voice behind you, saying, this is the way, walk in it." Isaiah 30:21

Dear God of all truth, I bless Your Holy Name. I lift You on high as I praise You today. I come to You with a humbled heart, bowing before You, asking that You direct my path. As I submit myself to You, I pray You let Your favor rest upon me. I ask for Your divine power over my life and that Your will be done on Earth as it is in Heaven. In Your word, it says *"The Lord will guide you always; he will satisfy your needs in a sun-scorched land and will strengthen your frame. You will be like a well-watered garden, like a spring whose waters never fail." (Isaiah 58:11).* I cast my cares upon You and rest, knowing all is well. May You cover me under Your blood and protect me from harm and danger. I ask that You intervene in my affairs, shut down whatever is not of You and create what is for me. Close doors so I can enter the right ones. When I am not getting what I want, when I don't understand or feel confused, please keep me reminded that You are guiding me. Help me to not be wise in my own eyes but give me Your wisdom, oh Lord, and help me to completely trust You with my life. If I lose my step, Dear God, thank You for not condemning me but leading me back on the right path. You know what and when to show me and it gives me so much comfort to know that You are standing by at all times and will never let me fall. Please continue to guide me into a life of fruitfulness and joy. In Jesus' name I pray, Amen.

Luke 1:79 – to shine on those living in darkness and in the shadow of death, to guide our feet into the path of peace.

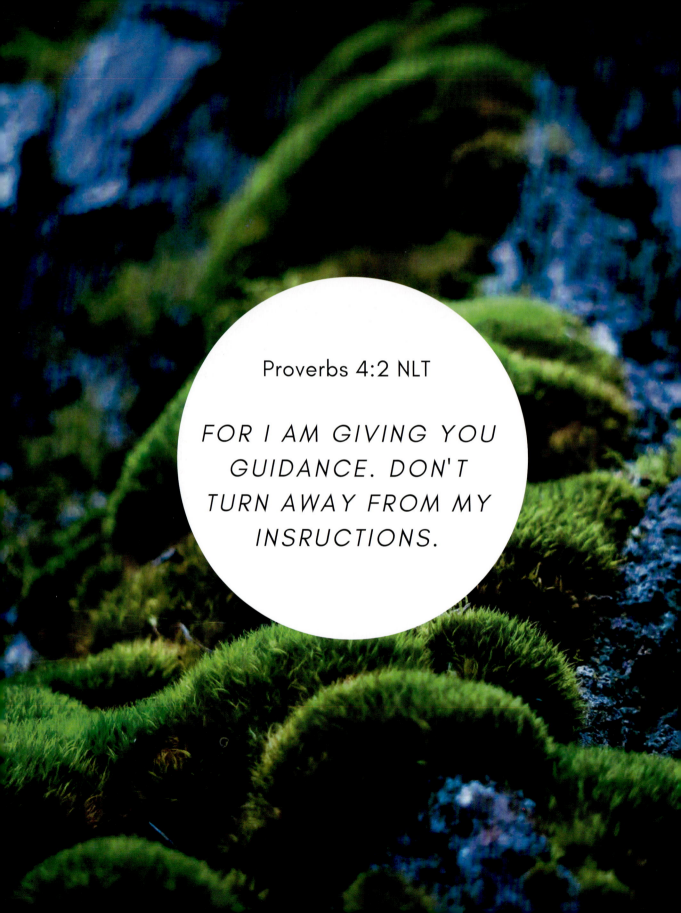

Proverbs 4:2 NLT

FOR I AM GIVING YOU GUIDANCE. DON'T TURN AWAY FROM MY INSRUCTIONS.

Reflection:

 WHICH AREA OF MY LIFE DO I NEED THE LORD TO GUIDE ME IN? AM I TRUSTING IN MY OWN WORKS OR IN HIS DIVINE GUIDANCE?

Protection

He will cover you with his feathers. He will shelter you with his wings. His faithful promises are your armor and protection.

Psalm 91:4 NLT.

PROTECTION

Thou a thousand shall fall at your side, thou ten thousand are dying around you, these evils will not touch you. Just open your eyes and see how the wicked are punished. If you make the Lord your refuge, if you make the Most High your shelter, no evil will conquer you; no plague will come near your home. For He will order his angels to protect you wherever you go. Psalm 91:7-11

My God my shield, my God who avenges, bless Your name. Thank you God for Your continuous protection in and around my life. Thank You for protecting me from things I am unaware of. Dear God, in the midst of difficulties and trials, it is comforting to know that I can trust You for help. Your word says that You will protect Your people and guard them along the way. Help me to remain steady through every storm in my life. Keep me reminded that my weapons of warfare are not physical, Lord, as the war has already been won. Please teach me how to win all my battles and to live in victory on Earth. When trouble comes my way, help me to not act out of character; to not defend myself but behave in a Godly way knowing that I am inaccessible to the enemy. God, You have given me authority over all the power of the enemy, so nothing can harm me. Let me always remember that You are more powerful than the Devil and when I make You my refuge, I have security. I pray and ask today, that You will protect me from anything that is not of You. Wrap me in Your love and power. Fill me with Your presence and Your anointing. Let Your angels encircle and encamp around me. Cover and shield me, God, as I take refuge in You. Just as Daniel survived in the lion's den, I trust that I will survive every snarl of the enemy. That same protection belongs to us today when we dwell in the secret place of the Most High (Psalm 91:1). Cover me with Your garment of light and let no darkness overtake me. Dear God, I pray You will never depart from me and nothing will divide us. As I walk in Your wisdom, please continue to direct my path each day. In Jesus's name, Amen.

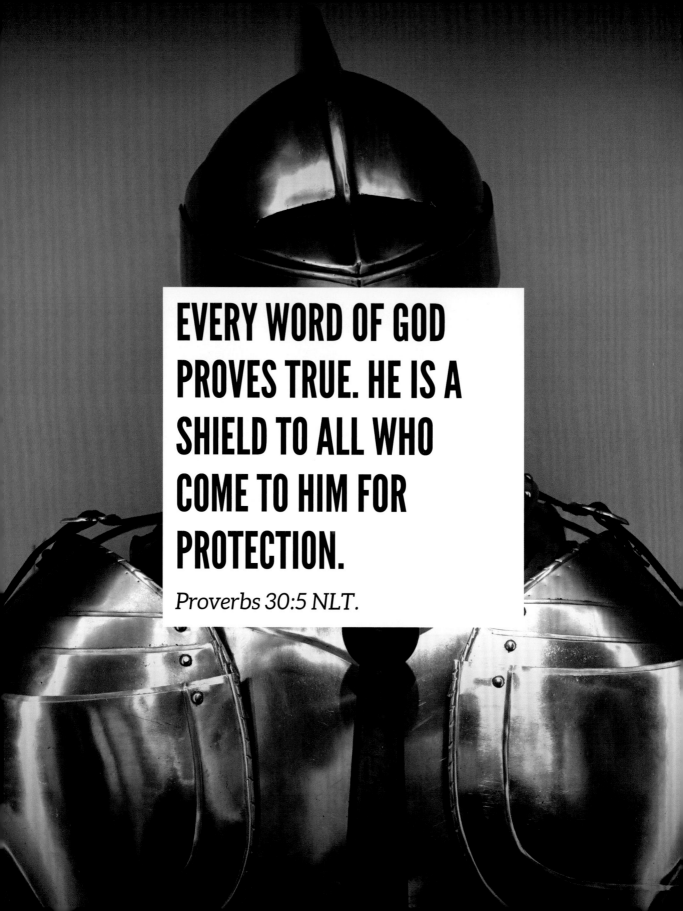

Reflection:

♥ AM I DEPENDING ON GOD'S PROTECTION OVER MY LIFE? DO I TRULY BELIEVE THAT GOD CAN PROTECT ME NOT JUST FROM PHYSICAL HARM BUT ALSO SPIRITUAL BATTLES? WHAT DO I NEED PROTECTION FROM? WHO DO I NEED PROTECTION FROM?

Blessings

May the God of your father help you; may the Almighty bless you with the blessings of the heavens above, and blessings of the watery depths below, and blessings of the breasts and womb.

GENESIS 49:26 NLT

BLESSINGS

For I am about to do something new. See, I have already begun! Do you not see it? I will make a pathway through the wilderness. I will create rivers in the dry wasteland. Isaiah 43:19

Dear God, Thank You for Your favor and protection over my life and for Your grace and mercy. Thank You for all the gifts You have bestowed upon me, both material and spiritual. Lord, help me not to be stuck on my past blessings or to live in bondage. Teach me to not hold on to blessings of the past but always look forward with a grateful heart, letting go of miracles from one season in order to receive a new thing for the next. Help me not to get caught up in the details of life and everyday situations but to remember to place my focus and attention on You, the Creator of All. I don't want to get used to a system but instead get used to You, God, my Source. If You have blessed me before You will surely bless me again. I ask that You will turn my barriers into blessings, my pain into power and my weakness into strength. Thank You for the uncountable times You have blessed me, open and closed doors, sustained me, protected and guided me. Teach me to live in the freedom that comes when I stop asking what and when and focus, instead, on Who. When I have internal conflict, please remind me that I don't need to know how if I know Who. You are my way maker, miracle worker, promise keeper and light in the darkness. You are the Alpha and Omega, the beginning and the end. Thank You for all Your blessings in my life, past, present and future. Lord as You have continually blessed me throughout my life, I pray that You will make me a blessing to others. Let all those I talk to, look at, walk pass, be blessed just because they came into close proximity to me. Continue to use me, God, for the works of Your Kingdom. In Your Holy Name I pray, Amen.

Galations 6:9

So lets's not get tired of doing good. At just the right time we will reap a harvest of blessing if we dont give up.

Reflection:

♥ AM I BLESSED? HAVE I MADE IT A HABIT TO COUNT MY BLESSINGS? AM I STUCK ON PAST BLESSINGS? IS THERE ANYTHING I WOULD LIKE TO ASK GOD TO BLESS IN MY LIFE?

Power

And because you belong to Him, the power of the life-giving Spirit has freed you from the power of sin that leads to death.

Romans 8:2 nlt.

POWER

"Now all the glory to God, who is able, through his mighty power at work within us, to accomplish infinitely more thane might ask or think." Ephesians 3:20

Dear mighty and powerful Father, How great are You! How majestic are Your ways, How glorious is Your love! Thank You for all that You are and all that You do. I know like You, dear Jesus, Your desire for me is to be great and powerful; I know you desire me to do remarkable works in Your Kingdom. I know that in order for me to do these things I have to go through a process to get to my promise. Lord, I ask that You will give me Your grace and power to withstand and endure, that I will not allow my circumstances to destroy my passion and drive, knowing that You are doing something amazing in my life. Help me to keep being tenacious and intense, to keep being passionate and excited about all that is coming; for my best days are not behind but ahead of me. Give me the patience and understanding as I am being pruned, developed and transformed into Your image and let my priorities and desires get into alignment with the Kingdom of God. I know sometimes, God, You will have to crush me and press me, in order to bless me. Help me to not let how I feel abort what I am called to do or to let my fear hold me back from my destiny. For You have not given me a spirit of fear but of power and of love and of a sound mind. To whom much is given, much is required. So today, Holy Spirit, I pray that by Your power You will empower me, by Your power You will strengthen me, by Your power You will equip me and teach me and by your power You will produce and bring forth fruit in every area of my life. I thank You. I love You. Amen.

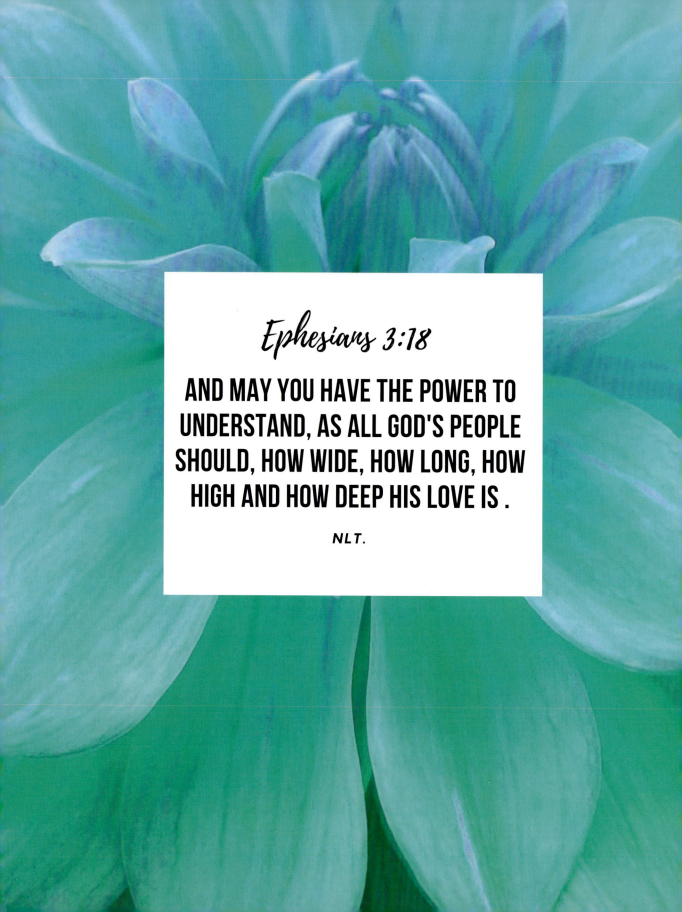

Reflection

♥ AM I DEPENDING ON THE POWER OF GOD OR THE POWER OF MAN? DO I HAVE GOD'S POWER TO STAND AND WITHSTAND? IF NOT, WHAT AREAS IN MY LIFE DO I NEED GOD'S POWER? WHERE DO I NEED HIS HELP THE MOST?

Obedience

Study this Book of Instruction continually. Meditate on it day and night so you will be sure to obey everything written in it. Only then will you prosper and succeed in all you do

JOSHUA 1:8 NLT.

OBEDIENCE

"...Anyone who loves me will obey my teaching. My Father will love them, and we will come to them and make our home with them." John 14:23

Dear God, In Your Word, it says we show our love to Jesus through obedience, and without obedience we have no more power than an unbeliever. Help me to become sufficiently sanctified by honoring and maintaining obedience to You, to live in Your word and to be filled with the love of God. Help me to be obedient, no matter what it costs me or how inconvenient it may be. Help me to trust You so much that I am willing to give up everything in order to serve You. Give me the obedience to say yes to Your will even when my heart says no and grant me Your peace in the midst of my sorrow. Let me not be afraid of Your voice but to recognise and listen keenly when You speak. I do not want to live a mediocre life but one that brings forth the greatness of who You are, in me. Help me to live my best life for You. Give me peace in knowing that I don't need to understand everything as long as it's a part of Your plan. Let obedience unite me with You and transform me into Your image. Matthew 16:24 teaches us that as Christians, obedience requires us to deny ourselves of our worldly desires. Open my eyes, ears and heart to You and lead me where You want me to follow. Guide me into Your plans and will for me as they are far greater than any will or plan I could ever imagine.. Give me the strength and power to just say yes to Your calling each and every time. Yes to Your will, Yes to Your plans, Yes to Your authority and Yes to Your purpose. In Jesus' name, Amen.

Obey me, and I will be your God, and you will be my people. Do everything as I say, and all will be well!

JEREMIAH 7:23 NLT

Reflection:

♥ IS THERE ANY AREA IN MY LIFE THAT I NEED TO BE MORE OBEDIENT? HAVE I BEEN DISOBEDIENT WITH ANYTHING IN PARTICULAR?

_____

_____

_____

_____

_____

_____

_____

BOLDNESS

"And now, O Lord, hear their threats, and give us, your servants, great boldness in preaching your word." Acts of the Apostles 4:29

My mighty and powerful Father, How great are You, how amazing are You? Almighty, omnipresent, omniscient, You are everlasting. You have no limits. How wonderful and encouraging it is to know that I am not a child of a timid and weak God. I was chosen and set apart to do big and bold things. Dear God, I know the devil is after me, after my walk with You, trying his very best to stop all progress and sometimes it may feel like time is running out or my window of opportunity is closing but, my God, the devil is a liar! I am a child of the one true God, I am a warrior and I will be bold like a lion. For me to become everything You want me to be, I pray for the strength to be bold, to do all the things You intended me to do. Give me the faith to take a stand in God and the courage to stand firm in the name of Jesus Christ. The devil and his army cannot stop what You have ordained for me. The crown of favor is upon my head and God will open doors that no one else can close. I have the God of Abraham, the God of Daniel and the God of Jacob and He has equipped and fashioned me to be more than a conqueror. I pray You will send Your angels to encamp around me, to protect me, to minister to and walk with me. I pray You will send Your Holy Spirit to dwell within me and guide me. I declare, today, that I will not be a spineless child of God, but just as Your son Jesus was bold, so shall I be. The devil will lose this battle because I will break chains and I will have the victory. I can do ALL things, through Christ who strengthens me. Amen.

Reflection:

♥ AM I BOLD IN THE KINGDOM OF CHRIST? DO I HAVE WHAT IT TAKES TO STAND FIRM IN MY BELIEFS? IF NOT, WHAT STEPS CAN I TAKE TO ENSURE I AM AND WILL BE?

_____
_____
_____
_____
_____
_____
_____

Faith

Dear brothers & sisters, when troubles of any kind come your way, consider it an opportunity for great joy. For you know when you are tested, your endurance has a chance to grow.

James 1:2-3 NLT.

FAITH

God of Heaven, thank You for Your love, Your kindness and Your faithfulness. Thank You for being the same yesterday, today and forever. Thank You, Lord, that Your word will never come back void and though You are a God of mystery, You have revealed Yourself as trustworthy. Dear Heavenly Father, I know it is impossible to be saved without having faith in You and without faith it is impossible to please You. I pray to have true faith in You, to have the assurance that the things promised in Your word are true; that the things revealed in Your word are true and that these things will come to pass. Help me to believe in that which I cannot see. I pray You will give me the kind of faith that weathers all seasons, that can stand on water in any storm; the kind of faith that is patient with abstruseness and a light when my world goes dark. When I am uncertain, help me to have enough faith to stay in Your will knowing that I have a certain purpose. I pray for the kind of faith that overcomes great opposition and that carries me through great trials. Help me to have the faith that pushes me forward even in the midst of uncertainty. Help me to have the kind of faith to know that even if my circumstances are working against me, my God is still working for me. Give me confidence, even when I am uncertain, to know that what I hope for is coming. Strengthen my faith so that I will always be obedient to You and trust in You, putting aside all self-reliance and interest. Let me fix my eyes on Jesus, knowing that He is the author and finisher of my faith as He sits at the right hand of the throne of God. In Jesus' name, Amen.

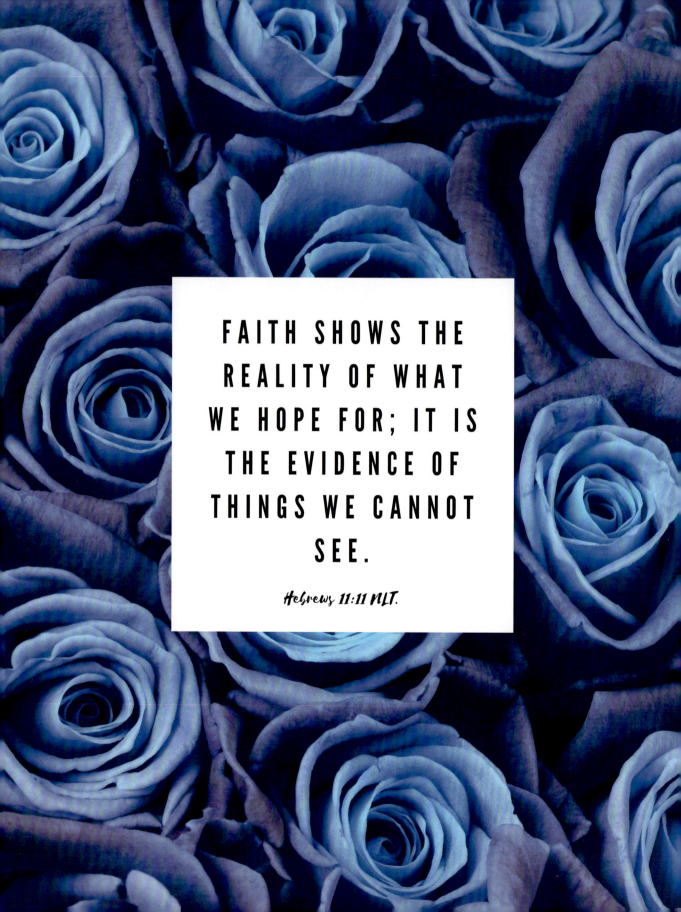

Reflection:

♥ AM I FAITHFUL? AM I LIVING AS A PERSON OF FAITH? WHAT CAN I DO TO STRENGTHEN MY FAITH IN GOD? DO I LET MY CIRCUMSTANCES OVERCOME ME OR DO I STAND FIRM IN FAITH?

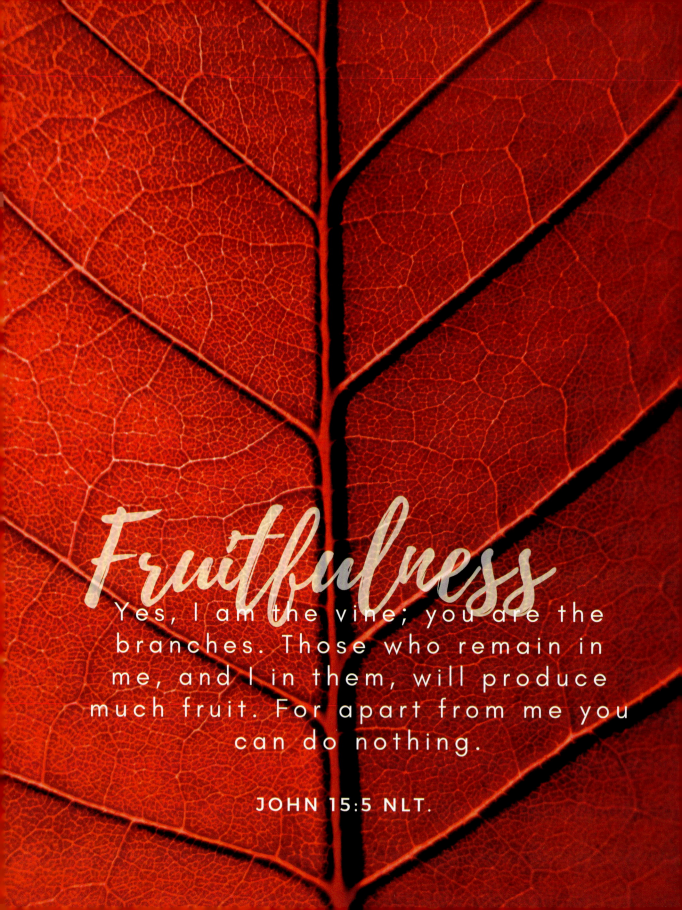

Fruitfulness

Yes, I am the vine; you are the branches. Those who remain in me, and I in them, will produce much fruit. For apart from me you can do nothing.

JOHN 15:5 NLT.

FRUITFULNESS

Everlasting Father, in Your word it says, " You will cut off every branch of mine that doesn't produce fruit and prune the ones that do, so they will produce even more." John 15:2

I pray, today, Lord, that as I focus on being stable in You and faithful to You, that You will make sure my life produces beautiful fruit. I desire to be a true representation and reflection of Jesus Christ. I pray that You will plant seeds in me that I will begin to grow. I pray, in this season of life, to be deeply rooted in You. Teach me how to focus on You as You prune the things out of my life that are hindering me from bringing forth the full potential I was created to reach. Give me the courage to make a clean break from everything that defiles and distracts me, both within and without. Dear God, I submit to the process - the cutting, the pruning and the crushing moments. Take away any runaway spirit from me and give me the grace to withstand. Help me to be stable and steadfast when I am confused, disappointed or hurt. Grant me Your grace to remain faithful, understanding, in purity and patience, in difficult and tempting times. Help me to trust that You are in control even in bad times. Forgive me for the times I have been unfaithful to You. I want to believe and live at the same level so please increase my capacity to produce more fruit. I want something sustainable in my life. Build me up so I can bear up under my blessings. Thank You for Your amazing faithfulness to me. Holy Spirit, I pray You will show me my full potential and my full capabilities as I abide in You and You in me. Fill me with Your spirit and power. Enable me to be truthful, humble and to love sincerely with a wide open heart. In Your Holy name I pray, Amen

Reflection:

♥ HAVE I GIVEN GOD PERMISSION TO PRUNE ME AND MAKE ME INTO HIS IMAGE? IS MY LIFE FRUTIFUL? WHAT CHANGES CAN I MAKE TO PRODUCE GOOD FRUIT?

Reassurance

Turn my eyes from worthless things, and give me life through your word. Reassure me of your promise, made to those who fear you. Help me to abandon my shameful ways; for your regulations are good.

PSALM 119:34-39 NLT.

REASSURANCE

"For this reason, brethren, in all our distress and affliction we were comforted about you through your faith." 1 Thessalonians 3:7

God of peace and all grace, today, I humbly come before You to feel Your love, Your peace and Your reassurance. Dear God, help me to get past trying to figure out why certain things happened in my life; help me to stop seeking closure or verification. Lord, with You, I don't need a reason; I only need Your revelation and reassurance. Dear God, help me to always remember Your love for me and to keep walking in Your truth. Whenever I am going through trial and tribulations in life, help me to focus on Your word. Help me to operate not by reason but by revelation. I know You are a God of righteousness, and all Your ways are good. I know You are with me, for me, before me and behind me; You will never leave me or forsake me. Faith may not always prevent me from getting hurt, grace will not always take away the consequence but, You, God, will always protect me and give me a place to rest. Keep me reminded that Your purpose is still intact even if my ship sinks. Position me not for destruction dear Lord, but for revival. Turn my mistakes into miracles and missions in Your Kingdom. Search my heart and fix my brokenness; remove any doubt or unbelief. Fill my cracks with Your truth and love. May Your Spirit fall fresh upon me each day and may Your Presence dwell within me always. In Your blessed name I pray, Amen.

Reflection:

♥ IS THERE ANYTHING I AM WORRIED ABOUT TODAY? DO I NEED GOD'S REASSURANCE OVER ANY SITUATION?

Peace

Then you will experience God's peace, which exceeds anything we can understand. His peace will guard your hearts and minds as you live in Christ Jesus.

Philippians 4:7 NLT

PEACE

God my provider, God of all comfort, My gracious God, thank You for Your peace that transcends all understanding. Thank You for washing my guilty conscience clean as I draw closer to You. Thank you for showing me that peace is not found in a place or in perfect situations but in You, heavenly Father. Thank You for standing with me in the fire, meeting me in the valley and guiding me through the darkness. Thank You for giving me the peace this world cannot offer or take away. Every step I take, every season I am in, You have been with me. Thank You for allowing me to walk in Your peace. Lord, when I forget, please remind me not to look for things I never lost, wondering in areas I am already freed from or going to other sources to find things that are already in my possession. In John 14:27, You said, *"I am leaving you with this gift – peace of mind and heart. And the peace I give is a gift the world cannot give. So don't be troubled or afraid."* Thank You, Father, for this undeserved gift of Your supernatural peace. Fill me with so much that I can access it at any time. Teach me how to use it in uncertain circumstances and teach me how to function in dysfunctional situations. Help me to focus on Who I am going with, rather than where I am going. Let my life be absent of inward turmoil regardless of what's happening on the outside. Let Your peace govern my emotions and my behavior. May God Himself, the God of peace, sanctify me through and through. I declare today that peace is my portion and as the peace of Christ rules in my heart, help me to spread Your peace to each and every one I come into contact with. Let Your grace and peace be with all who cross my path. In Jesus' name I pray, Amen.

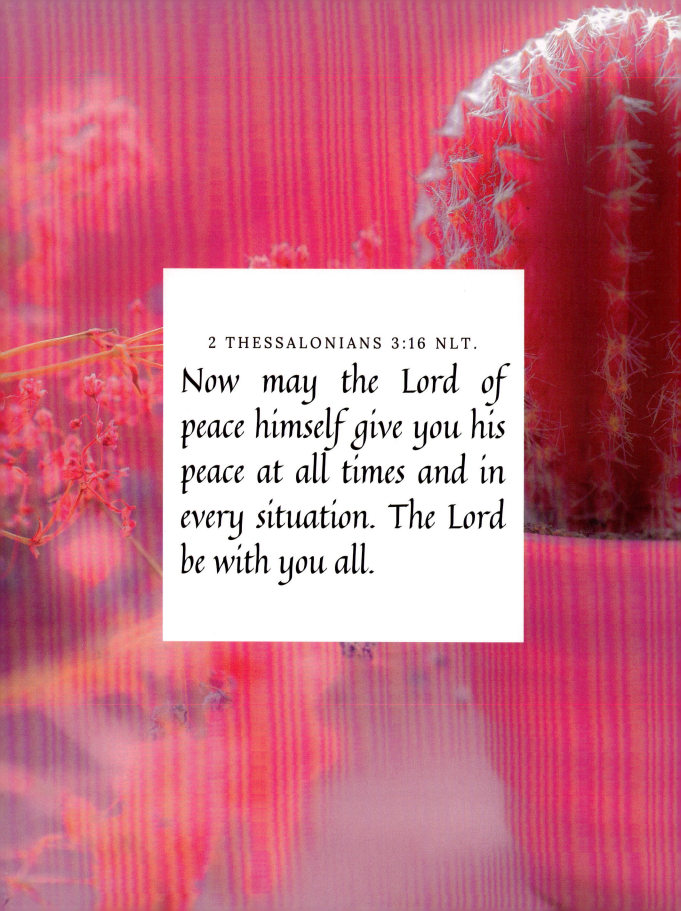

2 THESSALONIANS 3:16 NLT.

Now may the Lord of peace himself give you his peace at all times and in every situation. The Lord be with you all.

Reflection:

♥ DO I HAVE GOD'S PEACE WITHIN ME? AM I A PEACEFUL PERSON? DO I BRING PEACE WHEREVER I GO? IF NOT, HOW CAN I BE AT PEACE? HOW CAN I TRULY LIVE A PEACEFUL LIFE?

Presence

Let my soul be at rest again, for the Lord has been good to me. He has saved me from death, my eyes from tears, my feet from stumbling. And so I walk in the Lord's presence as I live here on earth.

Psalm 116:7-9 NLT

HIS PRESENCE

"This is my command – be strong and courageous? Do not be afraid or discouraged. For the Lord God is with you wherever you go." Joshua 1:9

Oh God of every moment, Thank You for Your word. Thank You for speaking directly to my heart. Thank You for giving me Your command and the comfort in knowing that when I obey, all is well. Thank You, God, that no matter what season of life I'm in, You remain the same. Thank You, that no matter who has left me, who has rejected me, who has forsaken me, as You were so You will always be. Thank You for never changing and that I can face all my circumstances with strength and courage. You will never abandon me even if I disappoint You. You will never leave me if I make mistakes, for Your presence is in me and with me always. Help me to enjoy each miracle and every gift as You give it and show me who You really are when I am going through transformation. Teach me how to come out better on the other side. Teach me how to go through situations as I focus on today's process and trust You with my tomorrow. Let what I know of You take over what I feel. Let me not waste today's strength on tomorrow's problems for You are already present in my tomorrow. I am beyond grateful that You go ahead of me. When I feel distant, Lord, use it to call me deeper in my faith and let it grow in unfamiliar places. Your word, Your truth and Your presence are the only things the enemy cannot take away from me. Let my priority be pleasing You, let it give me great joy and delight. Give me a heart that is open to You, a mind to understand You and a spirit that thirsts for You. As I prepare my victuals, let Your presence, that dwells within me, lead me to Your purpose. Bring me into a place I have never been, into a state I have never been. Move me to where Your victory is. In Jesus' name I pray, Amen.

Psalm 31: 20

YOU HIDE THEM IN THE SHELTER OF YOUR PRESENCE, SAFE FROM THOSE WHO CONSPIRE AGAINST THEM. YOU SHELTER THEM IN YOUR PRESENCE, FAR FROM ACCUSING TONGUES.

Reflection:

♥ DO I TRULY BELIEVE THAT GOD IS ALWAYS WITH ME? WHEN DO I FEEL GOD'S PRESCENCE THE MOST OR LEAST? WHAT CAN I DO TO FEEL CLOSER TO GOD?

Shepherd

The Lord is my Shepherd, I shall not want. He makes me lie down in green pastures; He leads me beside quiet waters. He restores my soul; He guides me in the paths of righteousness, For His name's sake.

Psalm 23: 1-3 NLT.

GOOD SHEPHERD

God my shepherd, Thank You for Your divine guidance in and throughout my life. Thank You for playing a big part in where I am today. Thank You for leading me in the path of righteousness. Dear God, You are the beginning and the end, the beginner and the finisher. Today, I place all my decisions and all my plans in Your hands. You are bigger than any decision I have ever and will ever make. Dear God, I know that You hear me. I know that You like it when I call on You. You hear my heart, my secret petitions and my unspoken words and it blesses Your heart. Help me to trust in You and to shift my focus from what I think I need to know to what you have instructed me to do and to know that even when my questions have not been answered, You will give me the wisdom I need. Give me the wisdom to search for You beyond my understanding. Calm my mind and spirit so that I am not tempted to go searching for answers or try figuring out things on my own, for that is not of You. Let me remember that You dwell in mystery, that You dwell in uncertainty; in the unknown and beyond my abilities and when I find myself in these places, remind me to rest in You. Dear God, I come to You with open hands, an open mind and an open heart. I have an expected end and destiny. Help me to make the right decisions to get there. Help me, Lord, not to go back to what I am being delivered from and I ask that You will use my bad decisions to deliver Your purpose. You have started a work within me and I know You will finish it. Help me to stop looking at what was and instead, to look forward to what You will have it be. I may not know Your plan, heavenly Father, but show me how to align with Your purpose. In Jesus' name, Amen.

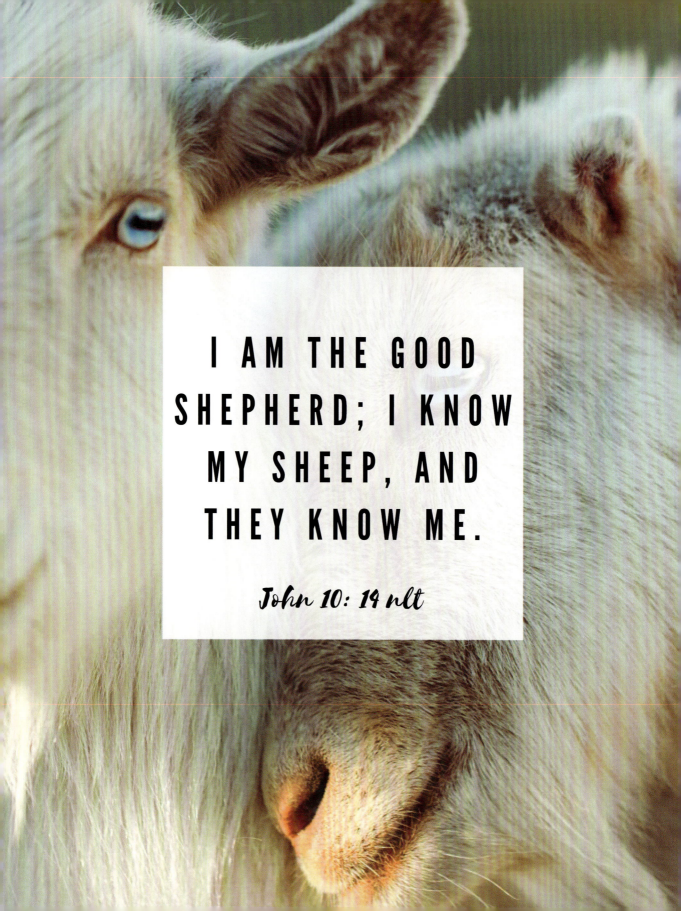

Reflection:

♥ DO I TRULY BELIEVE GOD IS LEADING ME INTO GOODNESS? IS THERE ANY AREA IN MY LIFE THAT I NEED GOD TO TAKE THE LEAD? HOW CAN I STRENGTHEN MY BELIEF IN GOD?

Joy

For the kingdom of God is not a matter of what we eat or drink, but living a life of goodness and peace and joy in the Holy Spirit.

ROMANS 14:17 NLT.

EVERLASTING JOY

Oh holy and glorious Father, Thank You for this day. Thank You for the breath of life. Thank you for another opportunity to spend time in Your presence and enjoy the goodness of who You are. Dear God, when I forget, please remind me, that joy does not come from what people say or think about me nor does it come from better circumstances. Help me to not chase a feeling, to stop comparing, to stop regretting and to stop looking too far ahead. Hebrews 12:2 tells us to fix our eyes on Jesus, the champion who initiates and perfects our faith. Because of the joy awaiting Him, He endured the cross, disregarding it's shame. Now He is seated in the place of honor beside God's throne. Fix my eyes on Jesus and help me to focus on what You are doing in this moment in my life. Give me Your wisdom to differentiate between joy and pleasure and between trial and temptations. Teach me not to accept what I should be resisting and not resist what I should be accepting. When trials come my way remind me to consider it pure joy, as the testing of my faith produces perseverance. When troubles come my way, God, I pray You will be my source, providing me with Your divine wisdom. Let me not settle for partial joy or attach my joy to temporal pleasure but to Your everlasting goodness. Let my joy be connected to You. Let me find joy in every season of my life knowing that I have a guaranteed outcome. Help me to not place my joy in the things I possess but where I am positioned. Set joy before me, dear God, and help me to be present in every moment with You. Let me find the fullness of joy in Your presence and let my joy flow not from what is but who You are to me. In Jesus' name I pray, Amen.

You will show me the way of life, granting me the joy of your presence and the pleasure of living with you forever.

PSALM 16:11 NLT.

Reflection:

♥ AM I DEPENDING ON OTHER PEOPLE TO PROVIDE ME WITH JOY AND HAPPINESS? AM I DEPENDING ON WORDLY THINGS TO MAKE ME HAPPY? HOW CAN I FIND EVERLASTING JOY?

Promises

And because of his glory and excellence, he has given us great and precious promises. These are the promises that enable you to share his divine nature and escape the world's corruption caused by human desires.

2 PETER 1:4 NLT.

CLAIMING GOD'S PROMISES

Dear Heavenly and Righteous Father, Today I pray that Your might will arise in me to lay hold of the territories You have promised us. I humbly bow my head before You and surrender myself to Your will. Lord, today I ask that You remove any and every distraction from my life that is hindering me from producing fruit in the Kingdom of God. I pray that You will give me a hunger and thirst for You like never before. I ask that You get me out of survival mode, knowing that I have an expected end, knowing that You make the impossible possible; knowing that all things work for the good of those who love You. I pray that I may operate in the Kingdom of God with courage. Give me the anointing for exploits, to do great things, manifest right now, heavenly Father, the spirit of wisdom. Dear Lord, I own the crisis presented before me right now. I will not negotiate my destiny, my future, my calling or purpose for this life. I am claiming my inheritance and possessions right now, Father, as You have given them to us. I will no longer slack, dear God, but will be fruitful right now, having visions and goals, working hard to increase and demonstrate the excellency of our Father in Heaven. May the God of Abraham, Isaac and Jacob keep me. May He bless and strengthen me to overcome every obstacle. May He lighten and carry my burdens and command angels to take up their positions around me. May my days be filled with clarity and may His peace obliterate all chaos. May lack no longer pursue me but may the favor of God fall upon me. May God uphold me and establish me, here, as in Heaven. May I be a light in the darkness and salt in the world. May I be planted by living waters and bloom with grace. May I find success in all that I do and may my days ahead be far greater than my days passed. All this I declare in the mighty name of Jesus, Amen.

Reflection:

♥ WHAT PROMISES ARE YOU CLAIMING TODAY?

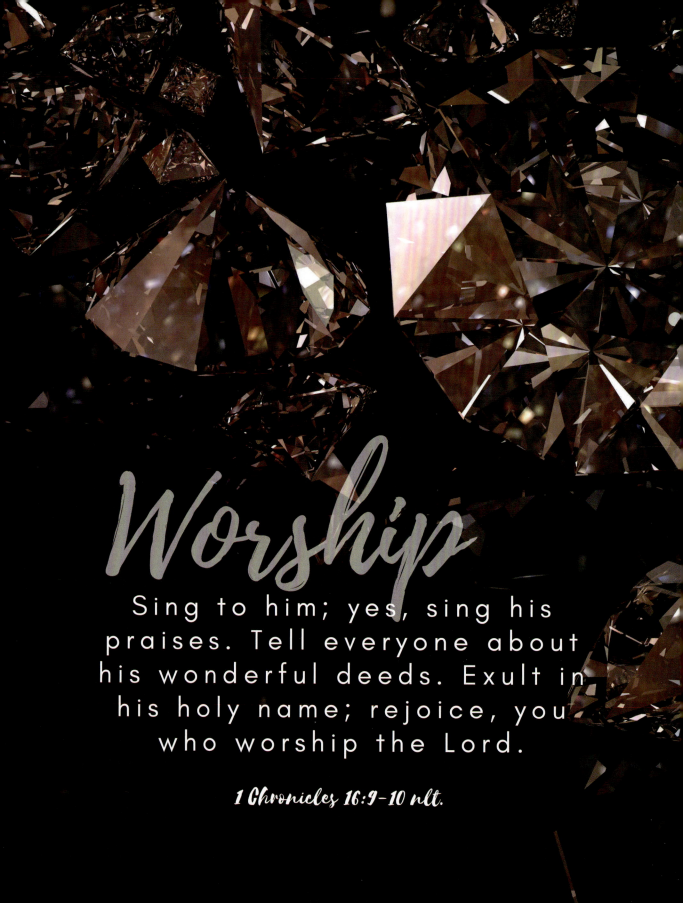

Worship

Sing to him; yes, sing his praises. Tell everyone about his wonderful deeds. Exult in his holy name; rejoice, you who worship the Lord.

1 Chronicles 16:9-10 nlt.

WORSHIP

"For God is Spirit, so those who worship him must worship in spirit and in truth." John 4:24

God of Heaven, God of Earth, God of All, How great Thou art? How great is Your grace? How overwhelming is Your presence? How unrelenting is Your love and how incomparable are Your ways? You are my shepherd, my provider, my comforter and my peace. You are my father and my best friend. You are worthy of it all, You deserve all the glory. Dear God, You have commanded us to worship You and I truly wish to understand what that means. Teach me God, how to worship You in spirit and in truth. Holy Spirit, I pray You will awaken my understanding of God's beauty, splendor and power. Stir up the desire within me to rejoice and celebrate Him with a grateful heart. Help me not to confine my worship to an expression of music and singing but to be sincere and motivated by my love for You and all that You are and have done. Worshiping You is the greatest honor, for You have never walked away from me, neither forsaken nor been too busy for me. Holy Spirit, as I worship with heartfelt commitment and faith, open my eyes to see and savor all that God is to me, through Jesus. Teach me to let my worship conform to the revelation of who and what God is. Let it be formed by the light of what is true and rooted to the realities of Your Word. Dear God, I am eternally grateful for the opportunity to show how much I value Your presence in my life. While I worship, help me to put aside everything and focus my mind on You; engage my heart, affection and totality of my being. All I want to be is with You forever. So pull me a little closer and take me a little deeper. In Your holy name I pray, Amen.

Reflection:

♥ DO I WORSHIP GOD OR AM I WORSHIPPING PEOPLE AND WORDLY POSSESSIONS? AM I WORSHIPPING THE LORD IN SPIRIT AND IN TRUTH? DO I KNOW AND UNDERSTAND THE TRUTH ABOUT GOD? IF NOT, WHAT STEPS CAN I TAKE TO GAIN MORE KNOWLEDGE ABOUT HIS TRUTH?

Believe

And it is impossible to please God without faith. Anyone who want to come to him must believe that God exists and that he rewards those who sincerely seek him.

Hebrews 11:6 nlt.

BELIEVE

Most High God, I believe in You. I believe that Your Son, Jesus Christ, died for my sins. I believe in Your Holy Spirit who dwells within me and shines through me. Dear God, I believe in You when my life is overflowing with blessings and I believe when it feels like a tornado has wiped my world clean. I believe; in good times and hard times, in times when everything is on track or when everything seems impossible. I know God that even though my plans may change, Yours won't. Let my relationship with You grow and develop, dear God. I want to follow You in the unknown, when You don't do what I expected You to do, when I am disappointed or heartbroken. Remind me that my negative circumstances still hold the potential to produce great purpose in my life. Even when the sequence of my life doesn't make sense, I believe the God, who lives outside of time, is eternal; my beginner and my finisher. Today, most Sovereign God, I pray You will expand my expectations to include the things I didn't plan for. I pray You release my mind and heart from the clutter of my own expectations. I pray You will break down all my invisible prisons – fear, doubt and unbelief. I pray You would enlarge the place of my tent, lengthen my cords and strengthen my stakes. Stretch my faith to a greater day, a brighter horizon and a higher hope. I pray You will not only meet but exceed my expectations. Deliver me from what I thought You were going to be and show me who You truly are. Your ways are so much bigger than mine and Your thoughts are so much greater. Remind me, God, that even when everything seems against me, You are for me and I pray and believe You will stand up to everything around me. Set up my stage, heavenly Father, and what the enemy meant for evil, turn it around for my good. Show Yourself strong in my life. I believe in You, God, and I believe in Your love for me. Thank You for all that You are and all that You do in and through my life.

Reflection:

♥ DO I TRULY BELIEVE IN THE FATHER, HIS SON AND THE HOLY SPIRIT? DO I BELIEVE GOD IS WHO WHO HE SAY HE IS AND WILL DO WHAT HE SAYS HE WILL DO? WHAT DO I NEED TO BELIEVE IN GOD FOR TODAY?

Child of God

Everyone who believes that Jesus is the Christ has become a child of God. And everyone who loves the Father loves his children too.

1 JOHN 5:1

CHILD OF GOD

Dear Father, Help me know to know You, the only true God, and Jesus Christ, the one you sent on Earth so I may have eternal life. Love me as You loved Your Son and let Your love for Him be in me and with me always. Teach me Your ways and give me Your divine wisdom and understanding so that I can be filled with joy and made holy by Your truth. Holy Father, please protect me by the power of Your name. Keep me safe from the evil one, and guard me so that I will not be lost. Give me the strength and capacity to complete the work You have given me, here on Earth, to bring glory unto Your Kingdom. Give me boldness and endurance to withstand every trial and battle, knowing all will be well. Grant me divine power that stands tall in the face of adversity and tribulations. Help me to trust and believe in You always, having faith much larger than a mustard seed. Give me Your comfort and peace beyond all understanding that I may rest in You, knowing who You are and that You are able and willing. Many are called but few are chosen so thank You for choosing me. I was always Yours. Everything I have is a gift from You and I have accepted them. I belong to you, so use me for you greater good. Shine in me and through me and bless me so that I may be a blessing unto others. Glorify me so I may bring back glory unto You and we can be One. May I experience perfect unity with You, that the world will know that I am a child of God. Amen.

dear friends
let us continue to love one another, for love comes from God. Anyone who loves is a child of God and knows God

1 John 4:7 NLT.

Reflection:

♥ WHAT AREA OF MY LIFE DO I NEED MORE OF GOD? WHAT CARNAL BEHAVIOURS DO I NEED TO CHANGE TO BECOME A CHILD OF GOD?

_____

_____

_____

_____

_____

_____

_____

GLORY TO GOD

God who created the Universe in beauty, God who governs this world with power and love; God who created me in His image; God who brought me back to life; God who wonderfully restored me in Christ; God who teaches, comforts, challenges me; God who leads me faithfully; God who sent me His Holy Spirit to empower me; God who finds a way back to my heart; God who hears my prayers, in Jesus's name; Thank You and let all the glory be unto You. Have all the glory in my life. Today, God, I praise You for who You are, not what You do. You are God when I don't sense You. You are God when I don't see You. You are God when I don't feel You. Even now You are Sovereign. Even now You are Holy. Even now You are working and showing up. I believe You are who You say you are. I believe You are the true and living God. Even when You didn't, You are. Even when I hoped for, You are. Even when I wished, You are. You are with me in the fire. You are with me in the storms. You are with me in deep waters. You are with me in the valley and You are with me in the dry places. Dear God, I know Your love is not proven in circumstantial evidence or by the way I feel Your presence but by the way I deal with Your perceived absence. Let my faith propel me to follow You anyway. Show me Your glory in a way I have never seen it before. Demonstrate Your power the way I have not yet experienced it. You are my God, the great I Am, the bread of life and the light of Heaven. I will continue to worship You. I will continue to be grateful. I will continue to have faith in You for I am restored, I am healed, I am delivered; I am saved and I have a testimony in Jesus' name. I invite You into every area of my life, all my secret and hidden places; resurrect the dead in me. My life doesn't end in death but in the glory and goodness of You, through the mighty power and anointing blood of Jesus Christ, Amen, Amen and Amen.

♥ DO I GIVE GOD THE GLORY OR MYSELF? DO I LIVE A GLORIFYING LIFE UNTO GOD? HOW CAN I LIVE SUCH A LIFE?

> The tongue has the power of life and death, and those who love it will eat its fruit.
>
> PROVERBS 18:21 NLT

Declarations

Declaration:

CHILD OF GOD

I AM A NEW CREATION, MY OLD HAS PASSED AWAY AND THE NEW HAS COME. I HAVE NO CONDEMNATION IN CHRIST JESUS. IN HIM I HAVE REDEMTION AND FORGIVENESS OF MY TRESPASSES. I AM FREE FROM THE LAW OF SIN AND DEATH. HE HAS DELIVERED ME FROM DARKNESS AND I AM TRANSFERRED INTO THE KINGDOM OF JESUS. I AM A CHILD OF LIGHT AND A CHILD OF THE DAY. I AM THE APPLE OF HIS EYE AND I AM FEARFULLY AND WONDERFULLY MADE. MY BODY IS A TEMPLE OF THE HOLY SPIRIT WITHIN ME. I HAVE BOLDNESS AND ACCESS WITH CONFIDENCE THROUGH MY FAITH IN HIM. HE GAVE ME A SPIRIT NOT OF FEAR BUT OF POWER, LOVE AND SELF CONTROL. I AM CREATED AFTER THE LIKENESS OF GOD IN TRUE RIGHTEOUSNESS AND HOLINESS. ALL THINGS WORK TOGETHER FOR MY GOOD. I AM CHOSEN AND I AM A CHILD OF GOD.

2 CORINTHIANS 5:17, ROMANS 8:1, EPHESIANS 1:7, ROMANS 8:2, COLOSSIANS 1:13, 1 THESSOLONIANS 5:5, ZECHARIAH 2:8, PSALM 139:14, 1 CORINTHIANS 6:19, 1 CORINTHIANS 12:27, EPHESIANS 3:12, 2 TIMOTHY 1:7, EPHESIANS 4:24, ROMANS 8:28, JOHN 15:16, JOHN 1:12

Declaration:

LOVE

I AM GOD'S MASTERPIECE, HE HAS CREATED ME ANEW IN CHRIST JESUS. THE LORD IS IN MY MIDST, HE REJOICES OVER ME WITH GLADNESS, QUIETS ME WITH HIS LOVE AND EXULTS OVER ME WITH LOUD SINGING. I AM PRECIOUS IN HIS EYES AND HONORED, HE LOVES ME AND IS WITH ME. HE STRENGTHENS ME, HE KEEPS ME AND UPHOLDS ME WITH HIS RIGHTEOUS RIGHT HAND. I AM ROOTED AND GROUNDED IN LOVE, FOR I KNOW THE BREADTH AND LENGTH AND HEIGHT AND DEPTH OF CHRIST'S LOVE FOR ME SURPASSES KNOWLEDGE. I AM FILLED WITH THE FULLNESS OF GOD. GREATER LOVE HAS NO ONE THAN THIS. NEITHER DEATH NOR LIFE, NOR ANGELS NOR RULERS, NOR THINGS PRESENT NOR THINGS TO COME, NOR POWERS, NOR ANYTHING ELSE IN ALL CREATION, CAN SEPARATE ME FROM THE LOVE OF GOD IN CHRIST JESUS LORD.

EPHESIANS 2:10, ZEPHENIAH 3:17, ISAIAH 43:4-5, EPHESIANS 3: 17-19, JOHN 15:13, ROMANS 8:35-39

FAITH

I HAVE THE ASSURANCE OF THINGS HOPED FOR AND THE CONVICTION OF THINGS NOT SEEN. I AM FULLY CONVINCED THAT GOD IS ABLE TO DO ALL THAT HE HAS PROMISED. I BELIEVE THAT HE EXISTS AND I AM REWARDED WHEN I SEEK HIM. I AM ALWAYS OF GOOD COURAGE, I WALK BY FAITH AND NOT BY SIGHT. MY FAITH RESTS NOT IN THE WISDOM OF MEN BUT IN THE POWER OF GOD. I WILL NOT ONLY DO WHAT WAS DONE TO THE FIG TREE BUT I WILL THROW MOUNTAINS INTO SEAS, I WILL UPROOT MULBERRY TREES AND PLANT THEM IN THE SEA FOR NOTHING IS IMPOSSIBLE WITH GOD. IN ALL CIRCUMSTANCES I CAN EXTINGUISH ALL THE FLAMING DARTS, I WILL FIGHT THE GOOD FIGHT AND TAKE HOLD OF ETERNAL LIFE TO WHICH I WAS CALLED. I HAVE BEEN SAVED AND AM JUSTIFIED BY MY FAITH. I AM MADE WELL AND MY SIGHT HAS BEEN RECOVERED. CHRIST LIVES IN ME, HE DWELLS IN MY HEART AND I AM ROOTED AND GROUNDED IN LOVE. THE LIFE I LIVE IN THE FLESH I LIVE BY FAITH IN THE SON OF GOD WHO LOVED ME AND GAVE HIMSELF FOR ME. I AM AN HEIR OF RIGHTEOUSNESS AND I SHALL LIVE. IT IS DONE FOR ME AS I HAVE DESIRED. WHATEVER I ASK FOR IN PRAYER IS MINE AND I WILL RECEIVE THEM THROUGH FAITH.

HEBREWS 11:1, ROMANS 4:20-21, HEBREWS 11:6, 2 CORINTHIANS 5:6-7, MATTHEW 21:21-22, LUKE 17:6, LUKE 1:37, EPHESIANS 6:16, 1 TIMOTHY 6:12, EPHESIANS 2:8-9, JAMES 2:24, MARK 10:52, GALATIONS 2:20, EPHESIANS 3:16-17, HEBREWS 11:7, HABAKKUK 2:4, MATTHEW 15:28, MATTHEW 21:21

Declare

The Lord's face shines upon me and is gracious to me, He lifts his countenance upon me and gives me peace.

@his_chosen_ones

Declaration:

PEACE

I AM KEPT IN PERFECT PEACE, EVEN MY ENEMIES ARE AT PEACE WITH ME. NOT AS THE WORLD GIVES IT TO ME BUT HE GIVES ME HIS PEACE THAT SURPASSES ALL UNDERSTANDING AND GUARDS MY HEART AND MIND THOUGH CHRIST JESUS. LENGTH OF DAYS AND LONG LIFE HAS BEEN ADDED TO ME, MY CHILDREN WILL BE TAUGHT BY THE LORD, AND GREAT SHALL BE THE PEACE OF MY CHILDREN. HE HAS LIFTED UP HIS COUNTENANCE UPON ME AND I LIE DOWN AND SLEEP FOR HE MAKES ME DWELL IN SAFETY. I AM REDEEMED FROM THE BATTLE THAT WAS AGAINST ME AND NOTHING CAUSES ME TO STUMBLE. HIS THOUGHTS TOWARDS ME ARE THOUGHTS NOT OF EVIL, BUT TO GIVE ME A FUTURE AND A HOPE. HE HAS GIVEN ME LIGHT IN MY DARKNESS AND GUIDES MY FEET, I GO OUT IN JOY. THEREFORE, HAVING BEING JUSTIFIED BY FAITH, I HAVE PEACE WITH GOD THROUGH MY LORD JESUS CHRIST.

ISAIAH 26:3, PROVERBS 16:7, JOHN 14:27, PHILIPPIANS 4:6-7, PROVERBS 3:2, ISAIAH 54:13, NUMBERS 6:26, PSALM 4:8, PSALM 85:10, PSALM 119:165, JEREMIAH 29:22, ISAIAH 55:12, ROMANS 5:1

Declaration:

FRUIT OF THE SPIRIT

I AM LOVE, I AM JOY, I AM PEACE, I AM PATIENT, I AM KIND, I AM GOOD, I AM FAITHFUL, I AM GENTLE, I HAVE SELF-CONTROL. I AM BORN OF GOD, I KNOW GOD THEREFORE I KNOW LOVE. FAITH, HOPE AND LOVE ABIDES IN ME. I WILL KEEP LOVING EARNESTLY AS LOVE COVERS A MULTITUDE OF SINS. I HAVE SET MY MIND ON THE SPIRIT. I HAVE LIFE AND PEACE. I CONTROL MY BODY IN HOLINESS AND HONOR. I AM WALKING IN A MANNER WORTHY OF THE CALLING TO WHICH I HAVE BEEN CALLED, WITH HUMILITY AND GENTLENESS, WITH PATIENCE, BEARING IN LOVE AND EAGER TO MAINTAIN UNITY OF THE SPIRIT IN THE BOND OF PEACE. I PUT ON LOVE WHICH BINDS EVERYTHING TOGETHER IN PERFECT HARMONY. I HAVE A SPIRIT OF POWER, LOVE AND SELF-CONTROL. I WALK IN A MANNER WORTHY OF THE LORD, FULLY PLEASING HIM, BEARING FRUIT IN EVERY GOOD WORK AND INCREASING IN THE KNOWLEDGE OF GOD. I AM PLANTED IN THE HOUSE OF THE LORD AND FLOURISH IN THE COURT OF MY GOD.

GALATIONS 5:22-23, 1 JOHN 4:7, 1 CORINTHIANS 13:13, 1 PETER 4:8, ROMANS 8:6, 1 THESSALONIANS 4:4, EPHESIANS 4:1-3, COLOSSIANS 3:14, 2 TIMOTHY 1:7, PSALM 92:13-14, COLOSSIANS 1:10

Declaration:

GUIDANCE

MY STEPS ARE ESTABLISHED BY THE LORD, I MAY FALL BUT I WILL NOT BE CAST HEADLONG, FOR THE LORD UPHOLDS HIS RIGHT HAND. HE MAKES STRAIGHT MY PATH. HE INSTRUCTS ME AND TEACHES ME IN THE WAY I SHOULD GO, HE COUNSELS ME WITH HIS EYE UPON ME. HE GUIDES ME INTO ALL THE TRUTH AND DECLARES TO ME THE THINGS THAT ARE TO COME. HE MAKES HIS WAYS KNOWN UNTO ME AND TEACHES ME HIS PATHS. THE LORD GUIDES ME CONTINUALLY AND SATISFIES MY DESIRES IN SCORCHED PLACES AND MAKES MY BONES STRONG. HE GIVES ME LIGHT IN MY DARKNESS AND GUIDES MY FEET INTO THE WAY OF PEACE. HIS WORD IS A LAMP UNTO MY FEET AND A LIGHT UNTO MY PATH. THE SPIRIT OF THE LORD RESTS UPON ME, THE SPIRIT OF WISDOM AND UNDERSTANDING, THE SPIRIT OF COUNSEL AND MIGHT, THE SPIRIT OF KNOWLEDGE AND THE FEAR OF THE LORD. I AM CONTINUALLY WITH HIM AND HE HOLDS MY RIGHT HAND, HE GUIDES ME WITH HIS COUNSEL AND HE WILL RECEIVE ME TO GLORY.

(PSALM 37:23-24, PROVERBS 3:5-6, PSALM 32:8, JOHN 16:13 PSALM 119:105, PSALM 25:4-5, ISAIAH 58:11, ISAIAH 11:2, PSALM 73:23-24)

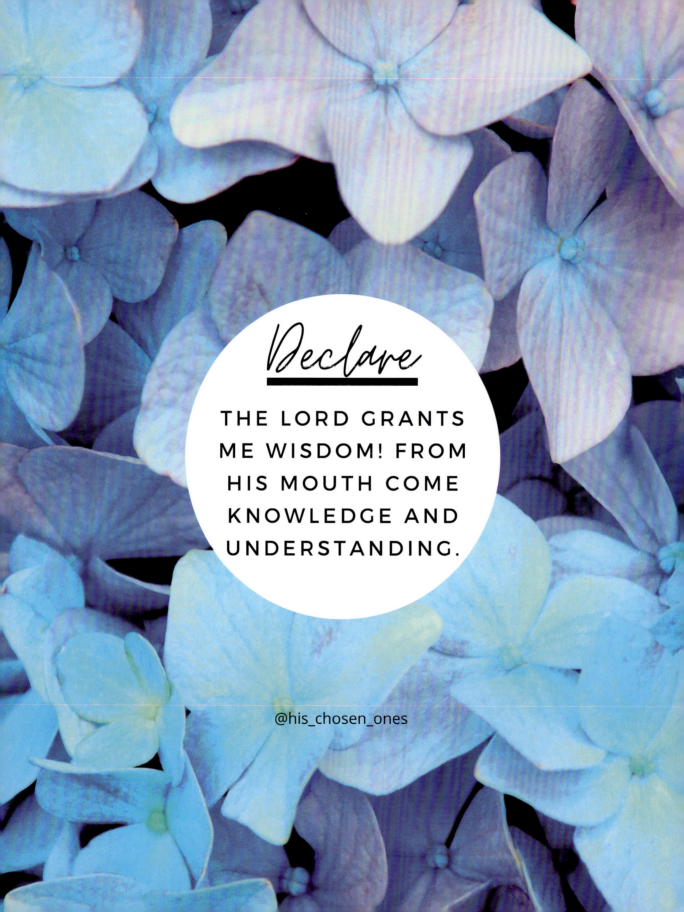

Declaration:

WISDOM

God gives wisdom generously unto me without reproach. He gives me wisdom that is pure, peaceable, gentle, open to reason, full of mercy and good fruits, impartial and sincere. I am blessed as God has given me wisdom and understanding, ways of pleasantness and peaceful paths. Wisdom rests in my heart and makes itself known in the midst of fools. He has given me a mouth and wisdom which none of my adversaries can withstand or contradict. My house is built on a rock. By God's wisdom and understanding my house is built and established, by His knowledge the rooms are filled with precious and pleasant riches. I am filled with the knowledge of His will in all spiritual wisdom and understanding. The Lord has given me a spirit of wisdom and of revelation in knowledge of Him, having the eyes of my heart enlightened so that I can receive understanding of the incredible greatness of His power.

(James 1:5, James 3:17, Proverbs 3:13-18, Proverbs 14:33, Luke 21:15, Matthew 7:24, Proverbs 24:3-7, Colossians 1:9, Ephesians 1:18-20)

Declaration:

LIGHT

I AM A CHILD OF LIGHT. I DO NOT WALK IN DARKNESS, I HAVE THE LIGHT OF LIFE. I SHINE IN DARKNESS AND THE DARKNESS CANNOT OVERCOME ME. I AM CLEANSED OF ALL SIN AS I WALK IN LIGHT. HE TURNED THE DARKNESS BEFORE ME INTO LIGHT AND TURNED THE ROUGH PLACES INTO LEVEL GROUND. I HAVE BEEN AWAKENED AND CHRIST SHINES ON ME, THE GLORY OF GOD SHINES UPON ME. I HAVE NO FEAR FOR THE LORD IS MY LIGHT AND MY SALVATION. MY LIGHT BREAKS FORTH LIKE DAWN, MY HEALING HAS SPRING UP SPEEDILY AND MY RIGHTEOUSNESS HAS GONE BEFORE ME AND THE GLORY OF GOD IS MY REAR GUARD. I AM THE LIGHT OF THE WORLD, A CITY SET ON A HILL, ON A STAND THAT GIVES LIGHT TO ALL. MY LIGHT SHINES BEFORE OTHERS, SO THAT THEY MAY SEE MY GOOD WORKS AND GIVE GLORY TO MY FATHER IN HEAVEN.

1 THESSALONIANS 5:5, JOHN 8:12, JOHN 1:5, 1 JOHN 1:7, ISAIAH 42:16, EPHESIANS 5:14, PSALM 27:1, ISAIAH 58:8, MATTHEW 5:14-16)

Declaration:

FAVOR

I AM BLESSED AND COVERED WITH FAVOR AS WITH A SHIELD. MY LORD HAS BESTOWED FAVOR AND HONOR UPON ME, NO GOOD THING HE WITHHOLDS FROM ME. LENGTH OF DAYS AND YEARS OF LIFE AND PEACE HAS BEEN ADDED TO ME, STEADFAST LOVE AND FAITHFULNESS WILL NOT FORSAKE ME. THE LORD'S FACE SHINES UPON ME AND IS GRACIOUS TO ME, HE LIFTS HIS COUNTENANCE UPON ME AND GIVES ME PEACE. I HAVE FOUND FAVOR AND GOOD SUCCESS IN THE SIGHT OF GOD AND MAN AND I HAVE OPBTAINED AN INHERITANCE IN CHRIST JESUS. I AM LIKE A WATERED GARDEN, WHOSE WATERS DON'T FAIL. HE HAS DELIVERED ME, HE PROTECTS ME, HE KNOWS ME BY NAME, HE ANSWERS ME, HE IS WITH ME IN TROUBLE, HE RESCUES ME AND HONOURS ME, WITH LONG LIFE HE SATISFIES ME AND SHOWS ME HIS SALVATION. HE MAKES ALL GRACE ABOUND TO ME. I HAVE ALL SUFFICIENCY IN ALL THINGS AND AT ALL TIMES, I ABOUND IN EVERY GOOD WORK.

PSALM 5:12, PSALM 84:11, NUMBERS 6:25-26, EPHESIANS 1:11, PROVERBS 3:1-4, ISAIAH 58:11, 2 CORINTHIANS 9:8-9

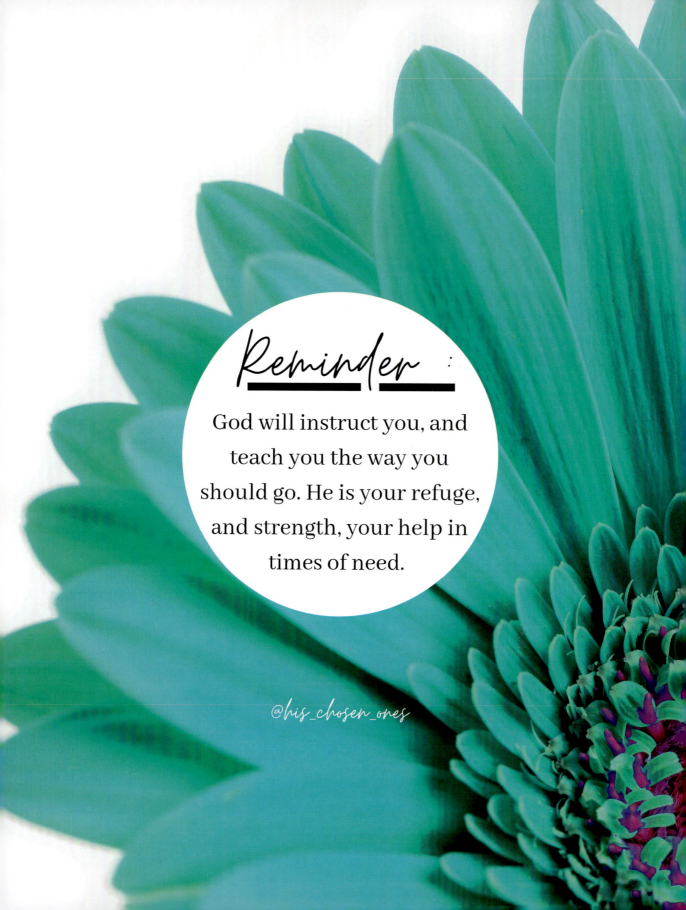

Declaration:

STRENGTH/VICTORY

GOD HAS GIVEN ME THE SPIRIT OF POWER, LOVE AND A SOUND MIND. I AM STRONG IN HIM AND IN HIS MIGHTY POWER. I HAVE VICTORY THROUGH MY LORD JESUS CHRIST. I AM MORE THAN A CONQUEROR THROUGH HIM WHO LOVES ME. IF GOD IS FOR ME, WHO CAN BE AGAINST ME? SIN HAS NO DOMINION OVER ME FOR I AM NOT UNDER THE LAW BUT UNDER GRACE. I HAVE NO CONDEMNATION IN CHRIST JESUS, THE LAW OF THE SPIRIT HAS SET ME FREE FROM THE LAW OF SIN AND DEATH. I WALK NOT ACCORDING TO THE FLESH BUT ACCORDING TO THE SPIRIT. NO TEMPTATION WILL OVERTAKE ME FOR GOD IS FAITHFUL AND WILL NOT LET ME BE TEMPTED BEYOND WHAT I CAN BEAR. I AM STRONG IN THE LORD AND IN THE STRENGTH OF HIS MIGHT. FOR HE WHO IS IN ME, IS STRONGER THAN HE WHO IS IN THE WORLD. I HAVE ON THE FULL ARMOR OF GOD, I AM ABLE TO STAND AGAINST THE SCHEMES OF THE DEVIL AND I AM ABLE TO WITHSTAND IN THE EVIL DAYS. FOR THE LORD MY GOD IS THE ONE WHO GOES WITH ME TO FIGHT FOR ME AGAINST MY ENEMIES TO GIVE ME VICTORY. THATS WHY I TAKE PLEASURE IN MY WEAKNESS, AND IN THE INSULTS, HARDHSIPS, PERSECUTIONS, AND TROUBLES THAT I SUFFER FOR CHRIST. FOR WHEN I AM WEAK, THEN I AM STRONG.

2 TIMOTHY 1:7, EPHESIANS 6:10, 1 CORINTHIANS 15:57, ROMANS 8:37, ROMANS 8:31, ROMANS 6:14, ROMANS 8:1-39, CORINTHIANS 10:13, EPHESIANS 6: 10 - 18, 1 JOHN 4:4, DEUTORONOMY 20:4, 2 CORINTHIANS 12:10

Notes

Notes

Notes

Notes

Notes

Acknowledgements

This book began very abruptly and it required way more than just my own hands to bring it to fruition.

First and foremost, I would like to thank God for changing my life completely, for bestowing upon me such an amazing gift that not only benefits me. This happened during such a stressful and confusing time in my life, but His grace was sufficient for me. I went from weeks of stress- related headaches, neck aches, back aches, sinusitis, acid reflux, and hair breakage, to peace, comfort, contentment and fulfillment in a matter of just three days. It was, and is such an unexplainable and overwhelming experience, and I pray that all my readers will experience God in all His splendours and glory. I thank Him for His guidance and direction every step of the way.

Thank you to my amazing friends Yoana Nikolova and Rianna Kerr-Impey for inspiring me to write this book. This entire journey began with one simple phone call that led me to fast with you two. Words cannot express how thankful I am to God for bringing you both into my life. The fellowships, the laughs, the bible studies, the tears, the jokes, the loving rebukes... I thank you for it all.

To my relentless mama, thank you for never giving up on me. Thank you for your constant and consistent prayers throughout my life. Your unconditional love and feedback during this process and journey were indispensable. I am eternally grateful for the unbreakable bond we now share.

To my dad, thank you for putting up with my stubborn and rebellious ways all these years and continuing to love me anyway..

Acknowledgements

To my dear Auntie Deborah Francis, thank you for your undeserving love. Thank you for your consistent prayers over me. Each time I called you to pray with me or for me you never hesitated, I cant express how grateful I am to have you in my life.

Sister Ingrid Bryan, thank you for the teachings and the explanations you so willingly shared. I appreciate the many phone calls, answering my birage of questions about the dreams I had, or to make sense of things I didn't understand.

Thank you to my sisters for being the best critiques!! Danielle, I love how I can trust your compliments and your criticisms, you will always be my go to girl. To my sister and editor, Christanya Julien, thank you for being such a genius, for tieing the shoelaces on my writing.. Kyrstle, thank you for being my shoulder to lean on throughout this journey. So appreciative of your hospitality, love and support. Thank you for being the sister I needed.

To my dearest friend Zoe Dawkins, thank you for being the best friend I needed. For always telling me the truth even when it hurts, for being my conscience when I seemed to not have one and for always steering me in the right direction. Thank you especially for always seeing the good and best in me.

And Finally, to all the beautiful people who, for whatever reason read my book, Thank You. I truly pray you were blessed and will continue to be blessed. I pray you will receive all the love, peace and joy that you so desire. Thank You.